# Corks & Forks

ROBERT FINIGAN

# Corks & Forks

*Thirty Years of Wine and Food*

SHOEMAKER SH HOARD

Library of Congress Cataloging-in-Publication Data
Finigan, Robert, 1943–
Corks & forks : thirty years of wine and food / Robert Finigan.
p. cm.
ISBN-13: 978-1-59376-099-1
ISBN-10: 1-59376-099-X
1. Gastronomy.  2. Wine and wine making.  3. Finigan, Robert, 1943–
I. Title.  II. Title: Corks and forks.
TX631.F524 2006
641'.013—dc22      2006008710

Cover art © The New Yorker Collection 1979
William Hamilton from cartoonbank.com
Book design by David Bullen
Printed in the United States of America

Shoemaker & Hoard
An Imprint of Avalon Publishing Group, Inc.

AVALON
publishinggroupincorporated

1400 65th Street, Suite 250
Emeryville, CA 94608
Distributed by Publishers Group West

10 9 8 7 6 5 4 3 2 1

For

Suzanne, my wife and my love

*and*

Robert Lescher

my friend, ally, and mentor for all my writing career

# Contents

❧❧

# Preface

❦❦

*I was gently introduced* to wine in college and much more seriously in business school, where one of my housemates was the son of a Bordeaux château owner and another the son of a wine collector in New York. The six of us came up with the now preposterous idea of advertising in the *Harvard Crimson* for a female undergraduate to cook for us five nights a week. After some amusing interviews from an ad which drew unexpected response, we settled on two Radcliffe roommates who had grown up around the world. They would plan fascinating menus, phone the grocer (who was always wary of our charge account) with their order, then one of us would pick them up after classes, pass by the grocer, and head home. The group of eight would enjoy an invariably delicious and often raucous dinner, after which we would more or less draw straws as to who drove the ladies back to Radcliffe.

Naturally, meals produced with such creativity deserved appropriate wines, but with limited budgets, we had to be exploratory with lesser known labels, nearly all of which in the Boston market of the time were French or Italian. Somehow, we got it done, although we had our share of losers among mostly winners, those sometimes amazing at their modest price points.

After school, we naturally went our separate professional ways. I joined an international management consulting firm, which stationed me, to my delight, in San Francisco, a city I had come to love after two summers of study at University of California–Davis. But assigned to an account with a major shipping company, I was away from home as much as not. That was not a problem, since my travel took me to so many intriguing places and allowed taking a bit of time off to learn more about the regional cuisines and wineries of France and Italy. It amounted to a fine practical education in what was good and what was not.

At home, I became intent on learning more about California wine, a burgeoning industry, since my exposure to the product had been limited. I started buying various bottlings, many of the names new to me, and I was surprised by the variation in quality. I was also experimenting with San Francisco's diverse mix of restaurants — French and Italian of course — but regional Chinese, Japanese, Vietnamese, Mexican, local seafood. I needed guidance to separate the downs from the ups, so I subscribed to the almost underground monthly newsletter *Jack Shelton's Private Guide to Restaurants*. An advertising professional, Mr. Shelton, irritated by what he saw as the connection between restaurant advertising in the publications that praised them, decided to go it alone, at first creating the newsletter from the basement of his home. He never made a reservation under his name and always paid in cash. And he always told it as it was, to the horror of some famous restaurants past their prime, and to the delight of small places worthy of discovery. He invented unbiased restaurant criticism as we know it now.

# Preface

Suddenly a bulb went on. I thought if Mr. Shelton is deftly guiding people through a mass of restaurants, why shouldn't someone be doing the same thing with the proliferation of imported and California wines? So on impulse, I called Mr. Shelton, and over lunch, we discussed the possibility of working together on a wine publication. Mr. Shelton said he couldn't because his advertising commitments were forcing him to give up the time-intensive restaurant guide. Besides, the most likely buyers wanted to start a wine publication of their own.

So another bulb flashed. Why not put together a small group of investors to buy Mr. Shelton's publication, and keep it going under my own name, and have Mr. Shelton control the marketing of the wine newsletter? That's just what happened, to a very pleasant result, over more than twenty years.

In the course of that time it was my good fortune to intersect with some of the major figures in gastronomy and wine worldwide, a journey that surely continues. But I thought it appropriate to take some time to describe some of the individuals who have been most central in my career, with immense impartment of knowledge and invariable graciousness.

*San Francisco*                                              *Robert Finigan*

# Corks & Forks

## Thirty Years of Wine and Food

# Discovering Bordeaux

## *Rolling the Dice*

*t was a warm* autumn morning when I turned north from
Bordeaux for my first visit to its famed vineyards and châteaux. Remarkably soon after leaving the classically handsome city, I was on the twisty rural route D2, swerving around
bunches of grapes dropped from groaning trucks ahead of me as
I noted the famous estates to my left and right, like diamonds on
velvet. It would have been a great experience had I been simply
a wine tourist.

But I was on a mission. A wine merchant friend in San Francisco was trying to decide what to do about the highly touted 1969
vintage. The Bordeaux wine trade was describing it as the finest
since 1961 and asking extremely high prices for the new wines,
as yet tasted by few outside the tightly knit Bordeaux wine community. Knowing I was about to make a business trip to Paris, my
friend asked if I could divert to Bordeaux for a few days and taste
the new clarets for him. His proposition was direct and appealing: He'd give me letters of introduction to the châteaux of most

interest to him in exchange for my tasting notes. I was both excited and flattered, since I hadn't yet embarked on my career in wine criticism.

My first stop was the handsomely turreted Château Palmer in Margaux, a Third Growth in the five-tiered and outdated 1855 classification of 1961 Médocs (see chapter 9). Palmer sounds English because it is, by heritage. Charles Palmer, heir to an English mail-coach fortune, was a general under Wellington and entered Bordeaux with the conquering army in 1814. Shortly thereafter he befriended, on a coach to Paris, Marie Brunet de Ferrière, a young widow who had inherited Château de Gascq in Margaux and wanted to sell it. By the time they reached Paris, Palmer had agreed to purchase the estate, and also to send her five hundred bottles of wine each year for the rest of her life. Would that we all could have such pleasant travel experiences.

With my introduction, I was welcomed politely if cautiously by the longtime cellarmaster, or *maître de chai*, Yves Chardon. After a few pleasantries, we went directly for a look at the '69 in question. In Bordeaux, wine in barrel is typically kept in shedlike buildings called *chais*. The cellar is usually under the house itself and the repository of past and future treasures for the proprietor's personal use. In visiting a *chai*, you notice right away that it is not very romantic as wine mythology might have it—no cobwebby nooks and such, as you'd find in cellars, especially in Burgundy—but rather a no-nonsense storage facility for long ranks of stacked barrels holding young wine. And it's chilly in there, coolest being best for wines moving slowly toward maturity.

And it's important to learn the protocol of tasting professionally. You examine the wine for color, swirl the glass to release either youthful aromas or bouquet (depending on the wine's age), then roll the wine over the tongue to understand its flavors and structure, and finally spit. In a formal tasting, you do this into a bucket, but in a *chai*, or for that matter a Burgundian cellar, you spit into a drain in the floor or into the pebbles around the barrels. It may sound impolite, but swallowing the wine is considered even more so.

M. Chardon had opened bottles of several Palmer vintages for me, but first we sampled the '69 from barrel. The wine was deep purple and cold, tannic from its high percentage of Cabernet Sauvignon, difficult to evaluate for the future because of its angularity and lack of forthcoming fruit. My impression fell more clearly into perspective in having tasted other Palmers, the '62, '64, '66—different in weight from one year to another, but not in charm, which I found the '69 lacking. I didn't like the '69 very much at all.

My next visit, at Château Léoville-Las-Cases, a bit north in Saint-Julien, took me to an estate of no particular architectural note, but surely of historical interest in that the vineyards during the eighteenth century were under the same family ownership as those that now comprise Château Palmer, just south. Also I was aware that Las Cases, like Palmer, felt it had been short-changed in the 1855 classification, from which Las Cases emerged as a Second Growth.

I was received by Michel Delon, third-generation member of the family that had gradually taken control of the estate. I knew Delon by reputation as general manager in title but wine master in fact; he knew me by no more than the letter which introduced me. Once again, we went straight to the *chai* and tasted the '69. Once more, under Delon's gimlet gaze, which became friendlier over the years, I concluded that I did not like this wine, for the same reason I hadn't liked the Palmer: clear but meager Cabernet fruit, texture verging on mean. Whereas the '61, '62, '64, and '66 vintages Delon and I tasted together were excellent, each in its own way, the '61 of course the shining classic.

The others of my first Bordeaux visits played out variations on the same theme. Whether at First Growths Château Latour in Pauillac, with long-time cellarmaster Jean-Paul Gardère, or at Mouton in the company of the legendary Raoul Blondin, who was already in charge of the Mouton cellars when Baron Philippe Rothschild took command in the 1920s, I came to the same conclusion. I found these initially praised '69s quite unsatisfying.

After three days of tasting at perhaps fifteen châteaux, I reviewed my notes over dinner at Dubern, at the time clearly the best restaurant in Bordeaux. I concluded I would not recommend these '69 clarets for my merchant friend's purchase, but I had the menu to deal with while thinking it over. I thought some tiny local shrimp followed by a *pièce de boeuf, sauce Bordelaise,* would be just right for the region and my good spirits in concluding a first visit to Bordeaux. When I ordered the shellfish, the waiter asked how many I would like, and I said perhaps two dozen. Polite but incredulous, he said "Two dozen *écrevisses,* and the beef after?" I said that would be fine, not realizing that I had mixed up *crevettes,* which are indeed the small ones, with *écrevisses,* or crayfish. On pride alone, I soldiered through both the crayfish and the beef, becoming a hero among the waiters but not feeling especially well on leaving this classic restaurant.

The self-imposed discomfort of that meal was soon forgotten, but not the experience of tasting the wines. On my report, my friend decided not to buy the '69s, a wise decision on his part, since the vintage soon was as widely discredited internationally as I thought it should be. I polished up my menu language, and I was on my way.

### ⌐ ALEXIS LICHINE ⌐

There are people one meets who are quietly important, self-important or rather magisterial. I would surely place Lichine in the latter category, though he could fit in any of the three. Born in Russia, he and his family fled to Japan via Vladivostok, on to New York and ultimately Paris at the time of the 1917 revolution, an odyssey indeed.

As I grew into appreciation of wine, I became aware of "Alexis Lichine Selections" as I was of "Frank Schoonmaker Selections,"

# Corks & Forks

both representing substantial presence as imports in the American wine market, and the two gentlemen business colleagues as well. But Lichine was not only a wine *négociant* and exporter, but co-owner of two classed growths in Margaux, Château Lascombes (1952–1971) with 51 percent participation, the rest from mostly American investors, and his beloved Château Prieuré, an old monastery and later winery. He purchased Château Prieuré in disrepair in 1951, restored it to excellence, renamed it quite properly with his name appended, and occupied it for the substantial part of the year when he was not in his grand Fifth Avenue flat.

Once my wine newsletter became established, I received many messages from PR representatives to meet with this or that person, to attend this or that event. I routinely declined, since I wanted no conflict of interest. But then came a call from Mr. Lichine's assistant saying that he was going to be in San Francisco to promote the newest edition of his *Encylopedia of Wine & Spirits*, and could we meet for dinner?

How could I ever pass that up? We met at The Mandarin, then the finest Chinese restaurant in the city, and immediately I perceived in the impeccably tailored Lichine a man of great good will much more interested in our meeting and our meal than in making a pitch for his book. Our conversation ranged widely, and in the course of it I mentioned I intended to spend the Christmas holidays in the Caribbean. "Then you must come to Barbados," he exclaimed. "I spend every holiday season there in a Sandy Lane house, with a good cook and my wines chosen for the climate. You really should come, though I have to warn you I'll have my two teenagers with me." I told him that this being November, I might not have much luck finding someplace pleasant in Barbados as an addition to my itinerary. "No," he said, "here's the name and number of my travel agent in New York. Call her tomorrow and she'll arrange everything."

So I did and so she did. At the incomparable Coral Reef Club, with its superb views, beach, and magnificent buffets, I was in Barbados heaven. I was hardly settled before Lichine called and asked me for lunch, a sandy walk away. He had the perfect Graham Greene Caribbean house, spacious, bright, and breezy. Lunch focused on the local flying fish, a solelike creature which either flies or jumps, but in any event moves around a lot, and was delicious with the Mâcon Blanc Lichine had selected. And the teens, Alexandra and Sacha (a Russian diminutive for Alexis, or Alexander) were worldly and charming. (You'll meet Sacha again in chapter 9.)

I was invited many times to the Fifth Avenue flat, where we would usually have a flute of Champagne before setting off for lunch or dinner, lunch commonly at one of Alexis's favorite homely Russian spots on the Upper East Side. In the flat, I noticed a photo warmly signed by Dwight Eisenhower. What I hadn't known was that having been drafted as a private in World War II, Lichine was identified as an expert in wine and food and was assigned as an aide-de-camp to General Eisenhower, who knew little about either subject, but had to entertain regularly the likes of Winston

Churchill. So entering the Army as a private, Lichine was mustered out as a major, I'm sure having selected many a fine bottle along the way.

And Alexis would have it no other way that every time I was in Bordeaux, I would stay at Château Prieuré-Lichine, where we dined well indeed, tasted and discussed at length possible blends from barrels of young wine which would eventually become the next vintaged release of Prieuré-Lichine. One time he suggested lunch at Château Mouton-Rothschild with his friend Baron Philippe Rothschild, later to become Robert Mondavi's partner in the exceptional Opus One project in Napa Valley.

On the way up to Mouton, Lichine told me a very funny story. As it happened, he was asked years before by the New York distributor of his wines to guide an important client, who had never been to France, through several important châteaux. Lichine was hardly enthusiastic but agreed. Wisely, he took the client to the *chais* of the Prieuré for a quick course in how one tastes in a French cellar—sniff and swirl the wine, roll it over the tongue, spit it into the gravel under the barrels. So off the next morning to Mouton. The Baron normally received in a lovely sitting room graced with one of the most beautiful Aubusson carpets I've seen. Pretty soon a server arrived with a tray of the Baron's personal Champagne reserve. The client took his glass, did the swirls, sniffs, and palate roll-arounds. In horror, Lichine saw what was coming next. "NO, HENRY," he hollered, "NOT HERE!"

On occasion, Alexis was not in Margaux when I was passing

through, but he generously offered the château as a place to stay on my own. I did that several times, at first to the gently expressed amusement of staff, who didn't quite know what to make of a guest in a grand home absent its owner or anyone else. But they were polite to a fault, and breakfasts were topnotch. But once there came a surprise.

It came on an evening when I was returning to the château after dinner, as sole occupant, to find it totally darkened, but the staff had told me where the key to the main door could be found, and I had it straightaway. However, in the pitch-dark house, I had no idea where the interior light switches were. I worked my way up toward my bedroom, but in the dark entered Alexis's instead. There was a shadowy apparition, moving slowly but not menacingly. Having never seen a ghost or even believed in them, I was motivated to leave for the next available room. When I later told Alexis the story, he responded with a deep chuckle. "Many monks were buried in these walls," he said, "and they do come around from time to time. Should have told you."

In 1989, I was asked to give a few wine lectures on a cruise ship which had a stop in Bordeaux, where I had arranged to debark. Naturally, in advance I called Alexis, whose assistant said he wasn't taking calls because of illness. But he cut in and picked up the phone. He sounded terrible, and said "They're telling me I'm dying of lung cancer from all my smoking, but I don't believe that. Tell me the name of your ship and I'll meet it." Not many nights later, a ship's steward asked to have a word with me during dinner, away from the table. "Sir," he said, "we've been asked to inform you that Alexis Lichine has died."

I had planned to transit Bordeaux, but instead I drove up to Margaux and the Prieuré. There, in a lovely part of the garden, was Alexis's bier, strewn with roses from those who had carried it from the village church to the château. I'm not a teary person, but I was then as I walked back to my car with a rose I pressed and keep to this day.

What a man. What a legend. What a legacy.

### ⌐ CHRISTIAN MOUEIX ⌐

Were you a first-time visitor to Bordeaux, a classically lovely city reflective in its architecture of its rise to prominence in the 18th century, you might be most drawn to the famed wine estates of the Médoc, on the Left Bank of the Gironde River. But you'd be missing the treasures of the Right Bank, especially the medieval hill town Saint Emilion. And the Right Bank is quite definitely, from a wine perspective, Moueix country. The family owns Châteaux Pétrus, La Fleur Pétrus and Trotanoy in Pomerol, Magdelaine in Saint Emilion and La Dauphine in nearby Fronsac. In 1981, Christian established Dominus in Napa Valley, a producer of Cabernet Sauvignons.

I have met and been impressed by Christian often, but my most memorable time with him was on an autumn day in 1981, a morning tasting at the Moueix cellars in Libourne followed by lunch at his parents' home.

# Discovering Bordeaux

Let me set the scene. Libourne is a sleepy town on the Dordogne River, which eventually flows into the Gironde, and it would be of no viticultural interest were it not the headquarters for important wine merchants, the Moueix family principal among them. Christian, tall, dapper, and cheery, had a special surprise at the tasting, that being the presence of Harry Waugh and his wife, Prue, visiting from England (see chapter 7). Christian showed us a brilliant range of recent vintages from Moueix properties, and then it was off to lunch.

The Moueix home certainly would fix your gaze on approach, accented by the background of the Dordogne. But on crossing the threshold with Christian and being greeted by his father, mother, and wife, it's a totally different matter. The late Jean-Pierre Moueix was a serious art collector, reflected by his pictures, but most immediately on entry in the foyer, by one of the very few casts of *Little Dancer, Aged Fourteen* of Degas.

Christian told me there would be a special wine at lunch, but I would hardly have expected the '61 Pétrus poured from magnum. Harry Waugh, seated next to my wife, leaned over and said "Young lady, taste this wine and think about it. You won't see much better in your lifetime." And he was dead right.

When Christian established his venture in California, he wisely followed the real estate mantra "location, location, location." There are few Napa vineyards comparable to Napanook in Yountville, originally the prime property of Inglenook, and Christian knew its history of having produced some of the finest Napa Cabernet

Sauvignons. However, oriented as he was toward Merlot, Christian had some early problems with Dominus, its initial Cabernets being on the tough side, but now they are simply splendid, flavory and elegant—in the latter sense just like their creator.

## ☞ BRUNO PRATS ☜

As I've indicated elsewhere, Bordeaux and London are connected on the wine side commercially, one being an important market for the other. But on the personal side, those at the top end of the London trade and their counterparts as directors of prime Bordeaux estates are far more similar than different. An ideal case in point is Bruno Prats, an elegant man who directed Château Cos d'Estournel, the family-owned Second Growth in Saint-Estèphe for years, until its recent sale.

Wines from this northern stretch of the Médoc tend to be hard with tannin in their youth, but Cos not so, especially under Bruno's regime, during which changes in viticultural and winemaking practices brought forth such fruity, supple, yet well structured reds well suited equally for near-term enjoyment as well as cellaring. In tasting with Bruno at Cos, which I've done many times, I made starred notes on the 1985, 1988, and 1990, among others, all wines with great flavor and breed.

Our tastings were always at Cos, as you'd expect, and Bruno is proud of its individuality, so many Médoc properties looking like one or another version of the White House. In contrast, Cos looks downright Indian, and for a reason. Louis-Gaspard d'Estournel, having acquired his vineyards beginning around 1810, saw a huge potential market for his wines in India, to which he made several trips. He was correct, surely in part because of the British presence, and a side effect was the design of Cos, a composite of design ideas gleaned from his visits to the residences of various nabobs, his customers. The huge and handsome carved doors leading to the *chais* once lived at the palace of the Sultan of Zanzibar.

Bruno lives at Château Marbuzet, which produces a regularly superb Grand Cru Bourgeois Exceptionnel Saint-Estèphe, and it really does resemble the White House in style and scale. In the course of a tasting at Cos, Bruno casually asked me where I was staying in Bordeaux, which was a perfectly nice place, but he shot back "Oh, no! The rooms are too small! Come to Marbuzet. You'll have the guest house to yourself, as long as you don't mind sharing it tomorrow with my sister and her Paris friends. And the housekeeper comes early, and will make you breakfast."

So there I was, alone in this comfortable house. The housekeeper arrived right on time and made a great breakfast, though startled to discover me there. Bruno's sister and her friends were utter delights, no surprise to me.

Since selling Cos d'Estournel, Bruno Prats has allied with the Symington family of Port fame to produce Chryseia, an intensely flavored dry red blend from the Douro, home to the most famed Ports. An interesting change of course for an inventive, creative man rooted in the traditions of Bordeaux.

# Corks & Forks

You're not alone if you think that the dust-covered 1855 classification of Bordeaux is outdated, and you'll see ample evidence
in chapter 9 of this book. Many have the misperception that the
classification was based on evaluations by skilled tasters, whereas
it was simply a scaling of recent prices created by brokers who
put together the five-tier system on the basis of their sales, at
the service of the home office in Paris planning an exposition at
which an "official" ranking of Médocs, in five groups, would be
announced.

Château Lynch-Bages in Pauillac didn't fare so well, classified a Fifth Growth, since at the time it wasn't commanding the
price enjoyed by its neighbors Latour and Lafite, or the nearby
Léovilles. But when my top-notch international tasting panel
reevaluated the 1855 Bordeaux classification in 1995, looking at
the vintages 1986 and 1990, Lynch-Bages emerged as eighth of
sixty-one classed Médocs, while its cousin Pichon-Longueville-
Baron was first, though deemed a Second Growth in 1855.

Virtually all this has to do with the dynamism and skills of
Jean-Michel, a man who can charm and impress you in the same
conversation. The family came to Pauillac from the central Pyré-
nées and eventually entered the insurance business, which in time
led to affiliation with AXA, the French insurance giant and major
source of capital for Cazes's interesting expansions.

Jean-Michel has added to his and AXA's portfolio Château

Cantenac-Brown in Margaux, a Third Growth in 1855 but having gone through a bad patch until Cazes took over, Château Petit-Village in Pomerol and the admirable Château Suduiraut in Sauternes. There's a wine from Minervois, at the western end of the Languedoc, which I've not yet tasted, and a very adequate simple red Bordeaux, which goes under the name Michel Lynch. There are interests in Portugal and Hungary.

I've saved the best for last. Think of the French country inn you've always dreamed of, and you'll find it at Château Cordeillan Bages, not far from Lynch-Bages and complete with a Michelin two-star kitchen, plus, as you'd imagine, a pretty spectacular wine cellar. The twenty-five rooms are spacious enough, and individually, creatively decorated. As for the food, keep in mind that in the southwest you're in foie gras, duck, and lamb country, but the kitchen puts a creative spin on these ingredients as well as others. I'd never stay anywhere else in the Bordeaux area, given a choice, though I'm sure that at peak periods reservations could be difficult, so think well ahead.

Jean-Michel has already achieved so much, with his constellation of prime wine estates, his beautiful inn, and superb restaurant, that one wonders what's next. Were I a betting man, I'd predict South America, but Jean-Michel is always given to surprise.

# Watching American Gastronomy Emerge

## Big Cabernets, Little Lettuces, and Influences Everywhere

*ow could I describe* the principal experience? Was it the first tasting of Warren Winiarski's 1973 Napa Cabernet Savignon, which captured first place in the famed 1976 Paris tasting? Was it a perfectly constructed meal by Jeremiah Tower at Chez Panisse, or an equally memorable one by Charlie Trotter at his eponymous restaurant in Chicago?

The only sensible answer is that each of these was an epiphany, but these three among others demonstrated the development of an American gastronomic consciousness that I had chosen to observe and comment on. San Francisco was a natural base from which to do that, but frequent travels elsewhere made it so abundantly clear that new thoughts about food and wine were emerging everywhere.

## Watching American Gastronomy Emerge

As someone new critically to the scene, I had to take stock of what those already established were saying. I found Craig Claiborne, the food doyen of the *New York Times*, rooted in '50s cooking, as I did James Beard, the latter more genial than the former. Bill Rice of the *Chicago Tribune* I thought was right on the money for both food and wine, and Frank Prial at the *New York Times*, principally of course for wine, his specialty. Harvey Steiman, from the *Miami Herald* to the former *San Francisco Examiner* and now at *Wine Spectator*, I thought absolutely on point in both wine and food criticism, and in the blending of the two, which has become his focus.

Of course I had to have my own look at what they were all talking about, just to compare. In New York, I found La Caravelle, La Côte Basque, and Lutece much overrated, rooted in the '50s, and then there was Le Cirque, the club of the rich and famous, a culinary French/Italian identity crisis directed by the sleek Sirio Maccioni, who knew his customers didn't care about the food anyway, as long as they were seated at the right table. All these restauarants are now shut, as better and more contemporary places emerged.

The gifted chef Daniel Bouloud must have understood that his talents were not properly appreciated at Le Cirque, which is doubtlessly why they are now expressed at Daniel, as well as at Café Bouloud, so personally and brilliantly. In so many other places, and in so many ways, a new generation of Americans was producing newly conceived restaurant food and exploratory wines congruent with the tastes of a new market. Charlie Trotter, in a Chicago historically tied to thick cuts of grilled red meat, brought to his quickly and justly famed restaurant a range of brilliant preparations often highlighting raw fish, and whether fish, fowl, or meat, Master Sommelier Larry Stone (now in Napa) could find just the right accompanying wine. Danny Meyer in New York, a newly fledged restaurateur in his late twenties when he opened Union Square Café in the '80s, brought to Manhattan the spirit and the kinds of dishes one would find in upscale Roman *trattorie*, with carefully selected wines to match, many of those not previously known here. And there's hardly been a spare table since the doors first opened.

Jimmy Schmidt, whom I first met through the redoubtable Madeleine Kamman, transformed the sleepy London Chop House in Detroit into a rightly acclaimed restaurant with wine list to match. Lydia Shire and Jasper White (both now on to other ventures) took the dining room at The Bostonian Hotel to justly deserved national acclaim, an element of its praise being mine and unexpectedly bestowed, having grown up around Boston, which had only recently developed a reputation for culinary creativity when I wrote about The Bostonian.

It was the same thing in San Francisco. Ernie's was thought the best in the city for too many years, featured in a Hitchcock film that pretty well places it in time and style: lots of dim light, red banquettes, and tableside presentations. La Bourgogne flew the French flag gamely, but serving mostly what Calvin Trillin would call "stuff with heavy." Hardly any Chinese restaurant was much better than what you'd find in, say, Indianapolis, surely including the socially lionized pan-Asian Trader Vic's. When I absolutely had to review the venerable seafood restaurant Spenger's in Berkeley, gymnasium-sized and perennially among the top-ten revenue generators of all American eating places, in response to my question of which fish were freshest, the cheery response was "all our fish is fresh-frozen!" And so the oxymoronic fish tasted.

Coming on to pick up the pace was a new generation. Jeremiah Tower transformed Chez Panisse in Berkeley from a simple café to an important restaurant and went on to establish his own Stars in San Francisco as the most plausible domestic alternative to La Coupole in Paris, and with mostly better food. Deborah Madison worked vegetarian magic at Greens. The freshest and most ideally prepared seafood began coming from Hayes Street Grill, near the Opera House, the creation of the very talented chef/writer Patricia Unterman.

And what were people drinking with this sort of food? Fewer and fewer followed their parents' preference in choosing liquor throughout a meal, or perhaps just water (at which prospect, in either case, Europeans would convulse). Wine choices were becoming ever more diverse, and very often made by individuals without traditional winemaking background.

Warren Winiarski, whose first-out-of-box 1973 Cabernet Sauvignon prevailed over prestigious Bordeaux competitors at Steven Spurrier's much-chronicled 1976 Paris tasting (s.v. chapter 8), had been a lecturer in political science at the University of Chicago. And Paul Draper, who for years has produced some of California's finest Zinfandels and Cabernets at Ridge Vineyards, holds a degree in philosophy from Stanford. The challenge to vintners in California, and to others within the United States, has been to match the best produced globally, and the most successful have done that. Warren Winiarski surely did, and so did Richard Graff, a Harvard music major and gifted organist who thought the right place for Burgundian-style Chardonnay and Pinot Noir might just be in the elevated stony soils of the Pinnacles National Monument in Monterey County. And he was right, at Chalone. A list of those who have been comparably successful would now run on and on, surely including the better properties in Washington, Oregon, and New York.

But it's also important, on the wine side, to think about the importers, merchants, and restaurant sommeliers, all of whose roles with regard to their customers have changed dramatically over the past generation or so. Time was, with the exception of such major top-line stores as Sherry-Lehmann in New York, that wine was a minor adjunct to liquor sales. And too often the wines, especially European ones, were mass-produced mediocre bottlings favored by importers who cared more about volume than quality.

There was a sea change in the '70s and '80s as small importers, invariably well traveled and focused on Europe, brought in wines principally from France, Italy, and Germany previously unseen on these shores. Kermit Lynch in Berkeley was one of the first and remains among the foremost, focusing on smaller estates in southern France and central/northern Italy. Neal Rosenthal in New York, as importer-retailer, and Robert Chadderdon, as importer in the same area, are at a comparably high level.

In a relatively short span of time, we've seen a large country never known for gastronomy become one that is. Our natural produce, always excellent, has been made better by a generation of farmers and ranchers with a collective eye toward maximum quality rather than production. And these materials have been brought to their best expression by a group of younger chefs, not trained in the European apprenticeship mode, but rather, for many, at such estimable schools as the Culinary Institute of America (both coasts, and the *good* CIA), the California Culinary Academy in San Francisco, and Dorothy Cann-Hamilton's French Culinary Institute in New York. And the wines simply get better and better, made by a cadre of vintners, some academically trained but almost none having learned at their father's or grandfather's knee, as is common in Europe.

I can only predict, given the positives in American gastronomy I've seen in my career, that, borrowing from Wall Street, the trend line should continue upward.

## ⌐ JULIA CHILD ¬

Like many, I used *Mastering the Art of French Cooking* as a bible while learning to cook. Not only did the recipes work, but exploring one after another constituted a sort of personal epiphany leading to lifelong love of cooking. Once or twice after a particularly successful effort, at least by my emerging standards, I thought about calling Mrs. Child, since she lived in Cambridge, I was in graduate school there, and her number was listed in the Boston-Cambridge phone book. But I never summoned up the courage to do that, and shortly thereafter I was immersed in business on the opposite coast.

Several years later, in transition from management consulting, I was entering the food and wine field by negotiating with Jack Shelton for purchase of his popular monthly guide to San Francisco restaurants. As it happened, Shelton had befriended Dorothy Cousins, Mrs. Child's sister and a fellow resident of Sausalito, a short hop over the Golden Gate from San Francisco. One day, to my surprise and delight, Shelton invited me to join him at the Cousins' home for an informal reception in honor of the visiting Mrs. Child.

Once we were introduced, I found Julia easy to know and totally without pretense, so very much in character from TV. We quickly fell into conversation about plain speaking in food and wine writing, a field we agreed was too populated with extravagant adjectives, and that began a dialogue which long continued. At the end of the evening, Julia—as she insisted from the outset that I call her—invited me to be in touch whenever in Boston, which next time there I did, and it resulted in the first of many memorable dinner invitations.

Anyone invited to the Childs' for dinner the first time might be a little apprehensive, but I wasn't because I already sensed how warmhearted Julia was, and I could even find their classic but secluded Cambridge home because I knew the landscape from college. What I didn't expect was the cast of characters in the Child kitchen, immediately familiar from TV with its precise peg-board outlines of where every pot and pan should be hung. Here was a wonderfully eclectic mix of Harvard academics, one or two Boston wine merchants, neighbors and friends, sitting on stools, chatting, enjoying each other's company. Paul Child, ever witty and dapper, was making drinks as I think most of us were wondering where Julia had gone.

Just then she burst through the kitchen door, bearing a huge pan with an especially ugly fish. "This is a *cusk*!" she exclaimed. "What do you think you do with a cusk?" I had the same reaction everyone else must have had—if she didn't know, none of us was going to be of much help. So an hour later we sat down to the most delicious fleshy white fish, roasted with summer herbs and basted with the same white Rhône with which we toasted our host and hostess.

But there was more. "I'm going to try you out on my nineteenth version of a low-fat *soufflé aux fraises*," warbled Julia. "The first eighteen were dismal failures!" The soufflé was a marvel of lightness and strawberry flavor, the soufflé base made with egg whites only, no yolks or milk, the trick being to control the amount of strawberry juice so that the fragile egg white mixture does not deflate to a watery mess. "Well, I might have gotten it right this time! What do you all think? And Paul, is there any more of that white Rhône? That was really good!" The recipe for this unusual soufflé later appeared in *From Julia Child's Kitchen*, preceded by a typically Julia discourse on how cane sugar is no different from beet sugar, no matter what the French say, even adding the chemical formula for sugar, to complete her point that sugar is sugar, and don't overthink it.

Another time in Boston, I was curious about a suburban restaurant operated by a prominent culinary figure as an adjunct to her cooking school. Local friends were raving about it, and I called the Childs to see if they'd like to join in. "We can't go there," Julia said sternly. "She's said some unpleasant things about us in the *Globe*. Very unpleasant." Having no axe to grind, I went and enjoyed a splendid meal. The next morning, my hotel phone rang bright and early. The familiar voice got right to the point: "Well, how was it?" asked Julia.

A couple years later Julia and Paul invited me to intersect with them on a France trip we were all making, appealingly at their second home in Grasse, in the hills north of Cannes and Nice. Grasse is best known as a source of perfume components, and you know why as you drive up the hills and inhale the breezes off the fields. Paul and Julia had purchased a classic Provencal *mas* close by the similar home of their friend and *Mastering* coauthor Simone Beck and her husband. Passage between the two houses was easy and often, and it was a pleasure for me to meet Simca, who struck me as a charmingly proper old-school French counterpoint to Julia's American exuberance.

# Watching American Gastronomy Emerge

For dinner at home, Paul first off had chosen a clean, fruity young rosé of the region, and we four had a chance to see and hear his comments on several of his exceptional paintings on mostly local themes. As always with Paul, it was impossible to predict where the conversation would lead, from painting and photography to wine or to anecdotes from his and Julia's OSS and later State Department years, their posting in Paris being where Julia was seriously bitten by the culinary bug. But it would always be fascinating.

On this evening, Julia had chosen to prepare, or for me unexpectedly to prepare with her, the seemingly fearsome Chicken with Forty Cloves of Garlic, an old and delectable preparation typical of this part of southern France. Chicken pieces are sautéed and then braised in white wine and stock on a bed of browned garlic cloves, the garlic sweetening in the process and melding with the stock to produce a smooth and subtle sauce. At a point over the rosé, Julia looked at me and said, "It's time to get going! You're peeling the garlic!" So we repaired to the kitchen, and I set about separating and peeling forty cloves as carefully as I could. When Julia was finished browning her chicken, she came over, after I had peeled perhaps fifteen of the cloves. With a pat on the hand and that great smile, she said "You know, dear, it doesn't have to be exactly forty cloves, and you don't have to peel them so very carefully. Don't you think?" I moved the process along, we had a great dinner, and Paul came up once again with a local red of uncommon distinction.

# Corks & Forks

More recently, we met Julia at what had become since Paul's death her new home in Santa Barbara, not terribly far from her native Pasadena. Many people think that her distinctive accent was of New England, but she was a Californian, and seemingly happy to be back on original ground. We had lunch at a simple local restaurant, where a familiar waiter greeted her with "Hello, Sunshine!" and as we drove her home, she invited us in to see what she called "my pad." It was smaller-scaled than Cambridge to be sure, but comfy and with a pretty garden and an efficient kitchen. The first thing I noticed there was the signature pegboard, scaled down, with an assigned place for every utensil.

I suspect that any meal prepared in Santa Barbara would have been just as memorable as those in Cambridge or the south of France, cusks and multiple cloves of garlic aside, because with Julia, it simply couldn't be any other way.

## ⁓ M. F. K. FISHER ⁓

You walk into the kitchen of the small Sonoma County cottage, and after an embrace from this diminutive, silver-haired lady you stand back and can only think how beautiful she is, mental images recalling from photographs how beautiful she had also been in her youth. Mary Frances had invited me for lunch.

Observers of the culinary scene often think of the most visible figures in the gastronomic world as distant icons, as some of them make themselves, but in my experience the best do not, names coming to mind being Julia Child, Jacques Pépin, Jim Beard. I quickly learned that Mary Frances was in that category.

# Watching American Gastronomy Emerge

Knowing her history in France and the United States, and her works from having read them, not to mention W. H. Auden's "I do not know of anyone in the United States today who writes better prose," I was anticipating that Mary Frances could be a bit distant in the company of a young writer.

Not so. As soon as I sat down at the kitchen table, she went to the nearby fridge and fetched a white, unlabeled and uncorked, and poured us each a glass. "Courtesy of my neighbors," she said. "Don't expect anything fancy here." She proceeded to mix a composed salad based on superb local greens dressed with a richly fruity olive oil. Heaven. Spontaneously, she put a small, soft hand atop one of mine and said, "You're very good, you know." I considered that one of the highest compliments I had, or have received.

If you're new to the world of M. F. K., you'll want to hunt up *The Art of Eating*, five of her best books collected between two covers. Hardly a cookbook, though there are recipes, this is such an observant and finely polished commentary about cuisine and wine that I often dip into it for the sheer pleasure of her company. It always brings me back to the warmth of that Sonoma kitchen with its simple salads, fresh young white wine, and sparkling conversation.

As an excerpt, which could be one of very many, in *Serve It Forth* we have her in an oyster restaurant in Dijon, in Burgundy, where she lived for a time. Her focus here, however, is on snails, a co-specialty as it would be in Dijon. Just follow her beautiful prose here. "Once I saw a woman eat seven dozen. It was *chez Crespin*, so she had already eaten more than that many oysters. She turned a purplish red. I have often wondered about her."

Pure Mary Frances.

⌐ JAMES BEARD ⌐

I was fortunate enough to meet this great bear of a man early in my career, in his East Village lair. That lovely smallish home, now the headquarters of the James Beard Foundation, which seems to exist principally to bestow awards from famous foodies to other famous foodies, was for me the site of many a hilarious kitchen lunch and the occasional special dinner in his small Asian-toned dining room.

One time, my wife and I met Jim in the kitchen for a preprandial glass of wine before proceeding to one of his favorite neighborhood bistros, where he tucked into *choucroute garnie*, the house specialty, served for two. The specialty of Alsace in northeastern France, Riesling-basted sauerkraut garnished with various pork products, it's delicious when well prepared but heavy going.

Not for Jim. He devoured the double portion with gusto, regaling us with stories of growing up on the Oregon coast, tales of an opera career that never took off, and delicious dish about high-profile chefs and critics whose work he considered markedly sub-par. Beard never did pull punches.

But he was the subject of some. One was his endorsement of products early in his career. For one thing, at the time he was not functioning as a critic but as a food writer, his work relegated to what were then called "women's pages," and he was trying to make a living, endorsements being a part of that. Another criticism has to do with allegations that he did not write such important works as *Theory and Practice of Good Cooking* and *American Cookery*, but that his long-time associate José Wilson did the work. If that is true, which I believe it is from Beard's own comments to me, I still have no problem. Many people have great knowledge but are not skilled writers, better at rough-drafts and dictation.

One of Beard's great strokes was taking under his wing Marion Cunningham, an immensely talented cooking teacher and writer based near San Francisco. I first met Marion when we were participants in a series of Saturday morning Chinese cooking classes beyond bizarre. I was so delighted when she told me that after participating in a series of classes with Jim in Oregon, he had asked her if she'd be interested in revising *The Fanny Farmer Cookbook*, first published in 1906. Marion jumped at it, did a brilliant job, and has had several cookbook successes since.

That's the essence of James: the biggest heart and most generous spirit, just as long as he thought you were both good and pleasant to be around.

### ⌐ JEREMIAH TOWER ⌐

Think Peter O'Toole, Graham Greene, then a dash of J. B. Priestley, a cocktail Jeremiah would surely enjoy, and there you have the man. Tallish and fair, with a carefully brushed head of reddish-brown hair, more fit than his years of cooking might imply he could be, Mr. Tower turns many heads, but were yours to be one of them, you'd better be as smart and witty as he is. He suffers no fools.

Jeremiah and I were classmates at Harvard College, fellow concentrators in English literature, but though it was a relatively small department, we never met there. He went on to Harvard's School of Architecture, I to Harvard Business School.

We intersected much later, having pursued careers neither of us would have contemplated, he a chef and I a restaurant and wine critic. Mr. Tower was transforming the Berkeley restaurant Chez Panisse from the simple student café it had been to the acclaimed destination it is now. I arrived for a review visit with my London friends Steven Spurrier and his wife.

At Chez Panisse, now as then, there's a set *menu du jour,* which will be your dinner. On this evening, the main plate was the classic *Gigot d'Agneau.* The perfectly pink slices of lamb presented to my guests could not have been finer. My lamb was a mess of gristly meat. I courteously asked the server to take the plate back, observing that the chef could not have meant to send that plate out.

In minutes he was back, with the same plate, and the terse comment "The chef says tough shit."

When Jeremiah and I became friends, he smilingly gave his version of the situation. According to him, Alice Waters, an original partner in Chez Panisse, had a tendency to overbook the restaurant and thereby overstress the chef and his crew. As Mr. Tower tells it, she had done just that on this evening, and while he was therefore running out of lamb, she cautioned him, under pressure as he was, to be sure my serving must be perfect. The result was on my plate, as retribution.

Remarkably, Jeremiah went on from his triumphs at Chez Panisse to a southwestern bent at Berkeley's Santa Fe Bar & Grill. Transmuting a sleepy locals' spot into a gourmet destination with a new name and new food was impressive indeed, as was his equally stunning makeover of the Balboa Café, a San Francisco neighborhood landmark best known as a haunt for career tipplers. When Mr. Tower took over the kitchen and installed a smart café menu and an excellent wine list, the barflies disappeared, replaced by a clientele far more fashionable.

Then came Stars, the fulfillment of Jeremiah's ideal of establishing a first-rate American bistro on the Parisian model. I knew the place, near City Hall and other government enclaves, as Bardelli's, a traditional Italian red-sauce restaurant favored by minor politicos.

Jeremiah, with his architectural eye, saw a sprawling, high-ceilinged space just yearning for transformation to something like La Coupole. And that's what he did with Stars, the name amusingly not from the cooking staff or the patrons, but rather from handsome star-patterned carpeting on which Mr. Tower was able to strike an attractive price.

But from the day the restaurant opened in 1984, stars of all sorts descended, locally, nationally, and internationally. Stars became one of San Francisco's toughest reservations, no matter what the day or time. Socialites, foodies, and political heavyweights jammed Stars for lunch, for evening drinks at the handsome long bar, and for dinner. A table on the dais overlooking the dining room, open kitchen, and bar was much coveted but couldn't be reserved by the random caller. You were either seated there or not, and Jeremiah directed the decisions, much in the manner of Sirio Maccioni at Le Cirque in New York or Jean-Claude Vrinat at Taillevent in Paris.

Jeremiah's menu, which featured his signature dishes as well as creative daily specials, reflected his eclectic tastes and what was best in the market. He'd want you to be seduced by his *Blinis à la Russe*, inspired by his Russian uncle, the fluffy little pancakes generously drizzled with melted butter and topped with the best caviar. Or you could choose pristine oysters, a superb seasonal salad, or various preparations of wild mushrooms. The bouillabaisse would take you directly to Marseille, though the fish was principally Pacific. Duck was always a specialty at Stars, especially as confit, and that led directly to a memorable cassoulet.

More simply, you could not miss with a classic steak and *frites* or with the best hamburger in town, something Jeremiah worked on until it was perfect, deciding that the ideal fat content of the meat had to be between 21 and 22 percent, not below and not above, and that none of the commercial buns he sampled matched the ones he had custom-baked.

As you might expect, the wines selected were just what should have been, from rustic but worthy bottlings from France, Italy, and California to many grander things, one's preference being the determinant in choosing from extensive options.

I think my single most memorable experience at Stars was one evening, just back from France and at Stars for dinner, when I chatted briefly with Mark Franz, Mr. Tower's right hand in the kitchen, and told him about a stunning dish I'd been served of scallop punctured with black truffle and served on a pool of *beurre blanc*. Mark nodded in agreement that what I described sounded great. Fifteen minutes later his version arrived as a surprise at my table, and it was better than what I had enjoyed in Paris.

And that reflects part of Jeremiah Tower's brilliance, in that he can not only create but teach others to perform close to his level. He eventually sold Stars, which withered without him, to pursue restaurant ventures in Seattle and Asia. Now peripatetic and working on book projects, his most recent *California Dish* telling maybe even more than you wanted to know about the California food scene from the '70s on, Mr. Tower offers his wry smile when asked about future ventures, literary or culinary or both. That response often indicates that something important is percolating.

### ⌒ BRADLEY OGDEN ⌒

Think American hotel dining and, for the most part, you think boring. When the new owners of the 1909 classic Drake-Wilshire bought it in 1981, they gave this venerable *grande dame* in the center of San Francisco a new name, Campton Place, 110 sleekly redecorated rooms, an elegant lobby lounge and a comfortable restaurant.

Presiding over the kitchen was Brad Odgen, a young culinary star who grew up in Traverse City, Michigan, went on to graduate with high honors from Culinary Institute of America in 1977, and in short order became executive chef of American Restaurant in Hallmark Center in Kansas City. He came to San Francisco and Campton Place in 1983.

That's where I met Brad, immediately impressed by his selection of the finest local seasonal ingredients simply prepared, an approach taken by other chefs who would have diners believe they had invented a concept in fact rooted in centuries of international cuisine. Brad has never gone that PR route, allowing his food to speak eloquently for itself. His "'aw, shucks" Midwestern manner belies his brilliance, both in the kitchen and in business, the latter amplified by his and wife Jody's partnership with Michael and Leslye Dellar, Michael a superb business person in the restaurant field.

From Campton, Ogden and partners went on to open Lark Creek Inn in Larkspur, just north of San Francisco in Marin County. This comfortable spot, especially appealing for its outdoor tables, speaks again about Ogden's focus on fresh, regional, and seasonal products, which you might see as Roasted Baby Beets (Marin Roots Farm), Humboldt Fog Goat Cheese, or Oak-Roasted Devil's Gulch Rabbit. Whatever you encounter will have been acquired freshly from small local producers and prepared creatively. The group opened another Lark Creek Inn in Walnut Creek, east of San Francisco.

One Market, in the heart of San Francisco's financial district, debuted in 1993 within an historic 1917 building. Chef Matt Christianson eventually took control of the kitchen at the restaurant Ogden founded and co-owns. His menu includes such things as shaved foie gras with hazelnuts, slow-cooked meats from the rotisserie, and a three-course bouillabaisse. If you can believe it, the delicious ice creams are made to order, courtesy of a magic machine.

Then there are the Yankee Piers, three at last count, based on the concept of the New England coastal "clam shack." That's where you'd stop on the way to Cape Cod for fried clams (particularly clam bellies, sounding gross but tasting delicious), or clam or lobster rolls. Ogden though a man of the Midwest, did his homework in New England and brought forth Yankee Pier. He took key staff with him on his research trips east and created excellent clones of standards, including a clam chowder that could well be the best to the left of Union Oyster House in Boston. Fish & chips, so often mishandled, is exemplary here, as are all the pristinely fresh local fish. The original Yankee Pier is very near the original Lark Creek Inn, while the other two are in San Jose and at the SFO United terminal.

Filling out the list of Lark Creek properties, Ogden has developed Parcel 104 in Santa Clara and Alterra in San Diego, both featuring his trademark American regional cuisine and American wines. Most importantly, he's opened the eponymous Bradley Ogden at Caesar's Palace in Las Vegas and has relocated there. Those in charge of local properties, however, appear to have kept up his high standards. But we'll miss Brad.

### ☞ DEBORAH MADISON ☜

If you're like me, you grew to maturity thinking of vegetarian or macrobiotic cooking as brown rice and bland. Then, in the early '80s, I discovered Greens and its chef, Deborah Madison.

I had to visit Greens because it was the first major vegetarian restaurant in San Francisco, and as a critic, I had to comment on it. An adjunct of San Francisco's Zen Center in a reconditioned government building, Greens, despite its beautiful Bay-view location, might have been another brown-rice outpost, but it wasn't, principally because of Ms. Madison.

Having been raised and educated in prime California agricultural areas, and drawn to Buddhist practice, Deborah, after a time at Chez Panisse, brought forth at Greens vegetarian creations the likes of which I surely had not seen before, and they are maintained by her successor at Greens, Annie Somerville. Think about (from *The Greens Cook Book*) such delights as Lentil Salad with Roasted Peppers and Mint, a Pita Salad Sandwich simply described but an astonishingly great combination of hummus, sweet bell pepper, crumbled feta, and minced Kalamata olives, red onion, and cucumber, together with a grace note of lemony vinaigrette. Then she created such pastas as Spaghetti Tossed with Eggs, Smoked Cheese, and Fried Bread Crumbs, an echo of the classic *carbonara*, and her pizzas topped with seasonal ingredients were always beyond reproach, as they remain at Greens. And no food lover could ever forget her Indian Vegetable Stew with Yellow Dal.

Several American chefs have been given and happily accepted kudos for introducing locally grown, organic ingredients to our national cuisine, a tradition of course rooted in centuries of international cooking, and for that matter in the heartland of America, where farming families raised what they ate. Deborah Madison and her cohorts at the Zen Center's Green Gulch Ranch in Marin County did essentially that, and the menu at Greens glowed with what they produced. Flavors jumped out with distinctive freshness but also in appositions that wouldn't have come immediately to mind.

I caught up with Deborah not long ago in Santa Fe, near where she now lives, since my wife and I were attracted by one of her frequent cooking demonstrations. She is obviously captivated by southwestern ingredients, very much like her contemporary and colleague Mark Miller (s.v.), and she's clear in saying that despite the titles of her books and her reputation, she's hardly a full-fledged vegetarian. And while at Greens, she helped importantly in development of a wine list both innovative and fairly priced, which it remains on both counts.

Deborah Madison, simply put, is a rare individual who radiates such beauty, both outer and more importantly inner, that being in her presence is even more enriching than is her captivating cooking.

## ⌐ CECILIA CHIANG ⌐

Cecilia, or Madame Chiang as she is reverentially called, introduced the greatness and diversity of Chinese cuisine to America. Growing up as the seventh daughter—not the most privileged position in a Chinese family—she learned at the foot of a father with a great love of food, and came to know that the "mandarin" tradition had to do with the highest level of dishes from various regions, not with a focus on just one, as might have been the thought of a young woman brought up elegantly in (then) Peking.

When the Japanese occupied Peking, Cecilia's father sent her and a sister to an uncle in Chungking for safekeeping. That involved a trek more or less comparable to walking from New York to Chicago. The two girls were fitted out with padded jackets to ward off the cold—but also lined with tiny gold bars to pay off bandits they might encounter along the way.

Eventually, Cecilia married a Chinese diplomat posted to Tokyo, where she opened her first restaurant, a huge success in its featuring the regional specialties of China, not so well known at the time in Japan. Once in San Francisco, she did the same thing, in 1968, with the appropriately named Mandarin.

I was attracted to this small storefront Chinese restaurant on

Polk Street, a shopping street between two upscale residential neighborhoods. The menu posted outside was intriguing because it listed specialties from (then) Peking, Shanghai, and Szechwan, districts whose food I didn't know. So I appreciated the new flavors of minced squab wrapped in crispy lettuce leaves, shrimp balls with ginger and rice wine sauce, smoked tea duck, red-cooked eggplant.

Then I began traveling to Asia on business on a pretty regular basis, and with multiple visits to Hong Kong and Taipei, I learned that while Chinese cuisine is regional by nature, in the major cities one can find representations of all the principal regional styles virtually next door to each other, just as it would be possible to find an excellent Milanese restaurant across the street from a fine Sicilian one in New York City. So you find the plumpest and most diverse variety of Shanghai dumplings (*dim sum*) at one place, and the best possible version of swiftly wok-fired Chungking beef strips just steps away. That was exactly what The Mandarin was exemplifying.

When I began my career in restaurant criticism, Mme. Chiang kindly asked me and a few friends to join her in a series of Tuesday-morning cooking classes at her now much grander Mandarin in Ghirardelli Square. I considered that a great opportunity; since I thought to write intelligently about Chinese cuisine in who knows how many situations, I ought to see it being produced at top level. That's what the young chef did, his every step and every word explained and translated by Mme. Chiang. The careful demonstrations were followed by ten-course luncheons of dishes totally different from those demonstrated in the morning, such as greaseless shrimp toasts, perfect in their simplicity, or seasonal garlic chives tossed with lamb, or red-cooked pork shoulder, almost always with uncommon noodle dishes, such as glass noodles with spinach, simply seasoned with dashes of soy and a bit of sugar.

Sometimes these meals were co-chefed by actor Danny Kaye, who as a Chinese cook of repute, often flew up from Los Angeles for the Tuesday occasions. Danny produced some delectable dishes and generally behaved amusingly and well, except for the time he became a bit too personal with the wife of a prominent Napa wine producer, who slapped him smartly, saying, "I don't care who you are! Don't do that!" And when I was groggily getting off an all-night San Francisco–London flight, there was Kaye, moving on the opposite walkway. To my astonishment, and to that of all others, he shouted "Finigan! Finigan! Turn back! There's no good Chinese food in London!"

When Cecilia Chiang sold The Mandarin, it was commonly assumed she would retire to her beautiful Marin County home. But retirement is not in Mme. Chiang's vocabulary. Shortly after sale of The Mandarin, she signed on as consultant to Betelnut in San Francisco, an unusual concept based on the idea of a Taiwan tea house. That means teas of course, and artisan beers, but particularly small plates of Chinese and other Asian food perfect for a meal on the light side. Dumplings are a feature, as are stuffed flaky pastries of various sorts, and seafood salads that change seasonally — and of course exciting noodles and stir fries, not to mention Cecilia's signature Minced Chicken in Crisp Lettuce Cups.

And sons Patrick and Frank have carried on the tradition in their own ways. Patrick controls the widespread and successful P. F. Chiang group of informal Chinese restaurants, while brother Frank — unlikely as it might seem — operates an outstanding *Italian* restaurant in Hong Kong. As the saying goes, it must be in the genes.

Mme. Chiang is ageless — one can only guess — but she brought Chinese cuisine to San Francisco, and really to America, at a level not before seen. I've learned an immense amount through her and made a lifelong friend besides.

### ROBERT MONDAVI

So much has been chronicled about Bob Mondavi's iconic career, it hardly needs reiterating. But some highlights do: his growing up in rural Minnesota, son of emigrant Italian parents seeking work there; graduation from Stanford in 1933; eventually joining the family business, the venerable Charles Krug winery in Napa Valley acquired by his family in 1943; his decision in the '60s to split off and establish his own Napa winery to produce wines above what he considered the standard at Krug.

That's when I first met Bob. I was curious about the construction of this first major winery in Napa since Prohibition, and while walking the site, I ran into Bob, who was doing the same thing. He couldn't have been more gracious, interested in my interest, even though at that point I had yet to write a word about wine.

Right away he began to expound on the kinds of wine he intended to make, often using the words "finesse" and "innovation." Regarding the latter, among many other things, Bob transformed Sauvignon Blanc, a white varietal principally made in California as a forgettable semi-sweet white, to Fumé Blanc, a name reflecting and its style resembling the Pouilly-Fumé of France's Loire Valley.

As for "finesse," as later more fully expressed by Bob, it had to do principally with what he considered the coarseness of too many Napa Cabernet Sauvignons. He was correct, as I also thought, that the tannin and alcohol levels were way too high, a result of so many winemakers wanting to make "monsters" to impress some critics and members of tasting groups.

Mondavi was seeking elegance in his Cabernets, comparable to what's found in the finest Bordeaux, and he made it happen in conjunction with his winemaker son Tim, and the prime fruit from the adjacent ToKalon vineyard. That's why it was no surprise to learn of the partnership of Bob and Baron Philippe de Rothschild of Mouton in the establishment of Opus One, surely among the prime Cabernet labels from Napa. Bob has long liked to use "sculpt" to describe his approach to creating red wines with finesse, especially Cabernet. What he's thinking about is Renaissance artists who took blocks of stone and fashioned something beautiful and gracious, which is what he's done with Cabernet, which can be crude and rough in the wrong hands.

Every now and then Tim has invited me to join his father and senior winemaking staff at the winery to taste blend alternatives for upcoming releases. It has always been fascinating, the exchange of opinions around the table illuminating. You could ask, "How could a critic be that close to a producer?" It's easy. Wines I tasted in progress at Mondavi I would later taste blind, on release, with comparable bottlings from others, so no name recognition could possibly be a factor in my judgment. But being a participant in these creative sessions has been a great learning experience.

Bob, in his nineties as I write, is a man not only of business and winemaking acumen but of great personal warmth, as all who have met him know well. I noted that particularly when I took my parents, on their first and only San Francisco visit, on a Napa trip, with a first stop at Robert Mondavi. I had intended this as a stop-and-go, my parents not being wine fanciers. But not the case. Bob and Margrit welcomed them to a small private patio, set out a small tasting, and conversed as if time were no object.

Bob Mondavi is very special, as are his wines. Knowing him, and them, surely are highlights in my career.

### ⌒ JOSEPH PHELPS ⌒

I first met Joe Phelps in the early '70s, when I was starting my publishing business and he his winery. Knowing he had taken a small Denver-based construction firm to national prominence and huge projects, I was expecting the high-adrenaline, quick-response American businessman.

Not at all. I found Joe an immediately charming, low-key person just delighted by how his handsome, wisteria-strewn redwood winery overlooking Saint Helena had turned out. He had been inspired by building two wineries, in Sonoma and Rutherford, for the original Château Souverain. That experience led him to establish his own, and build it.

For his original winemaker he chose Walter Schug, trained at the prestigious Geisenheim wine academy in Germany. Schug, who now has his own Napa winery, made for Phelps some of the best American Rieslings I had tasted, or have since. But Phelps, which no longer makes Riesling, has maintained the tradition by making an utterly delicious sweet wine from Scheurebe, a Riesling relative.

Joe Phelps wisely elevated Schug's associate, Craig Williams, to the top winemaking spot and in 1983 to vice president of production. Joe saw in Craig not only a superb winemaker but also someone who could work well with him in executing experimental ideas. One of those was the production of Syrah, not common in Napa, and surely the most notable being the development of Insignia. This Cabernet Sauvignon–Merlot blend, based on the Bordeaux model, has developed as one of Napa Valley's most prized reds, and is priced accordingly, as it deserves to be.

After an afternoon of tasting barrel samples and impending

new releases, Joe invited me up to his home above the winery, which it resembles in style. He went to his amply stocked cellar and brought up a bottle of nineteenth-century Sherry, saying as he poured our glasses, in his quiet way, "I think you'll like this." Well, yes. It was simply the finest Sherry of my experience.

And that anecdote, in an important sense, expresses so much about Joe Phelps. Construction magnate, yes; successful wine entrepreneur, yes; great gentleman, most importantly, yes.

### ⌒ ERNEST GALLO ⌒

You might think that meeting the head of the world's largest wine producer would be daunting, but I didn't find it so, since I found Ernest more avuncular than dictatorial.

Gallo wines by that time, in the late '70s, had begun to gather increasing respect, and Ernest was kind enough to invite me for dinner at his Modesto home. It wasn't so easy to find, but once I pulled into the driveway, lights came on, and security guards opened both doors simultaneously. I noticed that they were uniformed exactly as California Highway Patrol officers, except their shoulder patches were imprinted "E. & J. Gallo," with a bunch of grapes instead of the California State emblem. I asked one of them if it would be OK to leave my camera in the car, to which he responded, "If anyone comes close to this car, sir, he won't go much farther." (The Gallos take personal security very seriously, well aware of strikes against the Gettys and others of great wealth.) We had a jolly evening, nonetheless, accompanied by Gallo wines,

# Corks & Forks

which Ernest prefers above all others, unlike Bob Mondavi, who likes to have top-quality French or Italian wines on the table with his own. And yes, when we returned to our open car, my camera was right where I had left it, on the passenger seat.

In the early 1990s, I became director of the Classic Method/ Classic Varieties Society (CM/CV), a group of American (principally Californian) sparkling wine producers who believed use of "champagne" on an American label was simply deceptive, since Champagne must by definition come from the so-named delimited viticultural area northeast of Paris. The traditional method (CM) means fermentation of the wine naturally in the bottles in which it will be sold, not in vats and later carbonized much in the manner of a soft drink. There was also the matter of grapes (CV), which in Champagne must be Chardonnay, Pinot Noir, or Pinot Meunier, whereas "champagne" anywhere in the world can be made from just about anything, including the cheapest grapes available. Since at the time Gallo's flagship "champagne," André, had only bubbles in common with Champagne or our CM/CV wines such as Domaine Chandon and Domaine Carneros, he asked me down to Modesto to discuss the matter, and I assumed that would be one-on-one with Ernest—but not so.

The lunch was held in a large conference room, and aside from Ernest, across from whom I was seated at the long table, there were Julio, two or three Gallo sons, the PR director, and the top sales and marketing executives. Soon servers arrived, bearing trays of flutes of André. After we all sipped, Ernest looked across the table and asked, "Robert, isn't this as fine a champagne as there is?" The table fell silent. Thinking on my feet, or more accurately by the seat of my pants, I replied, "Ernest, I think it's a fine wine in its own category." The lunch was delicious, but as I was being peppered with questions from around the table, I couldn't devote full attention to it. As the plates were being cleared, Ernest glowered and said, "You didn't finish your lunch. Anything wrong with it?" Then, *sotto voce*, "Can you meet me in my office?" I had no idea what to expect.

"You did a good job out there. You almost had *me* convinced. What would you think about running our international operation in London?"

Naturally, I was both surprised and flattered, but I explained that I was happy with what I was doing and where I was living.

"Well, think about it, and call me if you want to discuss it some more."

Ernest long wanted to establish a more upscale Gallo image, which surely was accomplished with their Gallo of Sonoma program, involving massive earth moving and planting of prime vinestock. Gallo has been involved in Sonoma for more than seventy years as purchaser of fruit, but Ernest and Julio decided to create a new label, specifically Sonoma. That program, entrusted to Julio's grandchildren Gina and Matt, has been a huge critical success. I find the Chardonnay a special standout, in every year since its debut as Estate Reserve with the 1991.

Always carefully dressed and unfailingly gracious, Ernest is still *paterfamilias* in a huge business that has always been family owned. He has designated responsibility to such key people as Gina and Matt, and I'm sure to a small army of others at various levels of responsibility. But always, at the top of the pyramid, there's one man—Ernest Gallo.

⤳ KERMIT LYNCH ⤳

Thirty years ago, Kermit Lynch, a native of central-coast California, was manufacturing purses from remnants of elegant Oriental carpets and selling them to local boutiques. Betting on the belief that his developing passion for artisan wine could become a business, and favoring the aromas of wine over those of the glues used for the handbags, in 1972 he opened an eight-hundred-square-foot storefront shop in Albany, next-door neighbor of Berkeley. That's where I first met Kermit, as I was launching my own wine writing career, and where I came to appreciate both the wines and the man who was discovering them.

Lynch's store, now in Berkeley since 1981, is eight times the size of the Albany original, but the wines are still displayed in open cases, not on designer shelving. Names and prices are indicated on handwritten cards, not computer-generated stickers. Kermit Lynch wines are now distributed nationally through a sales office in Napa Valley and a ten-thousand-square-foot warehouse. On his own side, Lynch maintains a home in the Berkeley hills, and another near Bandol in the south of France, where he spends six months a year with his photographer wife, Gail Skoff, and their children. We enjoyed long conversations while we were both in Provence recently, conversations that extend from our initial ones of perhaps twenty-five years ago. And at about the same time, we connected for a great dinner at Oliveto in Oakland, directed by Paul Bertolli, unquestionably one of the most gifted chefs in northern California.

Lynch, a man of quiet charm and quick wit, totally lacking in the pretension that afflicts too many in the wine and food arena, could have fashioned himself as an icon for wine groupies. But he has never chosen to, preferring that the wines he selects speak for themselves. At the beginning, he dabbled in upscale Californians and a few Bordeaux in addition to his major focus on Burgundy, the Rhône, and the Loire. California went away, and only a few *petit château* Bordeaux remain on the list. Meantime, he managed to write *Adventures on the Wine Route* (Farrar, Straus, Giroux, 1988), to which I relate directly having had many of the same experiences Lynch describes, which we chuckled over together. (The book won the prestigious Clicquot award as best wine book of its year.)

Imagine that you're a thirtyish American in French wine country, trying to visit the best vintners and taste the best of their produce, in my case to write about them, in Lynch's case to induce their trust as their importer, and you as yet have little reputation. First step, crucial first step, is to establish credibility, and you do that through some mystical balance between good will and a demonstrated ability to taste. The first is easier than the second: Those whose wines you are tasting are almost always gracious, but they see right away, in your first or perhaps second taste, whether you know what you're about.

If you pass that bar, you're in for treats beyond barrel samples, mostly older vintages of the younger wines you've tasted, maybe even an invitation for lunch or dinner. But abstracting from that experience, pleasant as it surely is, you have to focus on what you have to know, whether importer or critic, as to how the wines relate to your experience with comparable regional wines, in both present and past tenses. It doesn't matter whether it's your first or fifth appointment of the day. You have to make almost instant judgments, and whether they are for writing (as in my case) or for purchasing (as in Lynch's), they are almost invariably respected over time by the vintners, as long as they perceive them as based on expertise and fairness.

That's exactly how Kermit Lynch has established and maintained the portfolio of wines he now represents. He tells you in his book about the fascinating idiosyncrasies of artisan winemakers, who for the most part are small farmers, not sophisticated international businessmen. Or women: He tells the story of the vintner in Gigondas who refused to sell him wine until Lynch learned from a Burgundian friend that he had made a mistake in not dealing directly with the wife, who managed the accounts. Lynch once shared with me a great tip, which is to discover small producers by seeing who's featured on local wine lists.

It's that sort of experience which leads to the kinds of superb wines Lynch has ferreted out from vintners virtually unknown in the United States. His Champagnes, for instance, come principally from two excellent properties at opposite ends of the Montagne de Reims, Lassalle in Chigny and Paul Bara in Bouzy. At $30 or so for the nonvintaged bottlings, both are revelations in contrast to the mass-produced brands, the Lassalle more delicate, the Bara elegant as well but more forceful. They are just about the best I know among the smaller producers. Nearby in the Loire, Lynch has found one of the best dry Chenin Blancs, that of Château d'Epiré in Savenièrres ($15 for the '98) as well as the Cabernet Franc–based Chinons of Charles Joguet, equally delightful in the bracing rosé ($14) or the red "Jeunes Vignes" ($14), soft and supple, just right with a light chill.

Kermit rightfully enjoys a great reputation as a selector of Burgundy, and that skill also extends to Beaujolais, where he represents, among others, the silky and classically fashioned Côte de Brouilly of Château Thivin as well as the Morgon of Guy Breton for fleshy and just plain delicious, their moderate high-teens prices defended by sheer quality.

And the portfolio of Burgundies themselves is beyond reproach. When Lynch first started explorations there, he ran into the same two problems I did. First, the best producers made something very different from what came from most large shippers. Many of the latter firms believed the English market, and later the

American, wanted Burgundy to be perceived as more full-blooded than Bordeaux, so they often stretched the accurate product with richer (also simpler and cheaper) reds from southern France, or as legend has it, northern Africa. Pinot Noir when well handled simply does not yield that sort of wine, so tasting from barrel the most outstanding wines from the finest properties revealed a quite different style of Pinot, far more accurate to the intrinsic character of the grape, and in the best cases, reflective directly of the *terroir* where the grapes were grown.

The second problem was a variation on an old theme—is what you see what you get? In Burgundy, a vintner will always offer a sample from a superior barrel, but what you eventually find in bottle when the wine is shipped may not recall your original tasting note at all. That is less likely to happen in Bordeaux, where the young wine you sample from cask is already a blend of varieties, and barrel variation is minimal, in comparison with what happens from barrel to barrel with the single varieties, Chardonnay and Pinot Noir, most common to Burgundy. That reality was made especially clear to me when I wrote disparagingly about an esteemed Vosne-Romanée, making clear the disparity between what I had tasted in the cellar and what I found in a California-purchased bottle of the same wine. When next I visited the vintner, he somewhat abashedly confessed, "What I sent to the U.S. was not what you tasted here," and a bottle of the top-quality wine he handed me—same labeling as the one I had purchased in

California—confirmed what he said. The way Kermit Lynch gets around that problem is to insist on tasting from many barrels and reserving the specific ones he wants. Were a vintner to deceive him, there would not be another order.

So the Lynch list features such stellar Burgundies as the Chassagne-Montrachets of Michel Colin, the Meursaults of Guy Roulot, the mostly forthcoming Gevrey-Chambertins of Philippe Rossignol and the more brooding ones of Domaine Maume, the utterly correct Nuits-Saint-Georges of Domaine Chevillon. Keep in mind that these are personally selected lots, pick of the litter, so to speak, and therefore in the $30–$80 range, rightly so. But here's a little secret you may find useful in browsing Lynch's list. The quality standards of these producers are such that the bottles a notch below their own absolutely top selections are sold as "blanc" or "rouge," wines that would be toward the top of any-one else's heap. Lynch snaps up these wines, and that's how you can find such treasures as Bourgogne Blanc of Roulot ($20 or so), pure Chardonnay bliss without weight; Bourgogne Rouge (around $15) or Côte de Nuits Villages (roughly $20) of Rossignol, both clearly Gevreys, the latter rather richer than the former.

Lynch's wine journeys took him south to the Rhône, and he forged relationships with, among others, such legendary masters of Syrah as Gérard Chave, whose Saint-Joseph is offered at around $20, only just in the shadow of his famed Hermitage, and the pro-fessorial Auguste Clape, whose Cornas is without a superior and which shows well in the mid $30s. Farther south still, Lynch fell immediately in love with Lucien and Lulu Peyraud of Domaine Tempier in Bandol, which produces vibrant but hardly weighty reds, focused largely on Mourvèdre. Kermit liked what he saw *chez Peyraud* so much that he not only imported the wines but purchased a nearby property where he spends that half-year in Provence. There were winemaking properties not so far away, and Lynch struck up relationships with some of his favorites. That's how we have access to such excellent, really well made examples from the likes of Saint Martin de la Garrigue, Château La Roque and Domaine d'Aupillhac—all at $10 or so.

That continuous search through outstanding regions of the south yielded a special prize for Lynch. He had established a representation for the superb Châteauneuf-du-Pape of Domaine du Vieux Télégraphe, and in that context, he and the Brunier family decided on a small joint venture in Gigondas, near Châteauneuf. We had a prerelease bottle, richly colored and vibrantly fruity, at dinner in Oakland, and the rich, supple quality of the wine, in its appeal and accuracy, brought me back to the first experience I had with Gigondas, by the small carafe and as a neophyte, with lunch at a sidewalk café in Saint-Germain-des-Prés. It was just so perfect with the *salade niçoise* alongside. When I described that distant experience to Lynch over dinner, he said, with a chuckle, "I think this one is that sort of wine." And he was exactly right. It's now in release.

The back label of all Kermit Lynch wines reads, "Good wine is a necessity of life for me—Thomas Jefferson." Kermit would be the last to put himself on a pedestal with the third president, but they surely share the same sentiment about wine.

## ☞ THOMAS KELLER ☜

It was late on a lazy summer Napa afternoon and on my way home after tasting barrel samples from a few local wineries for the annual "Wines in Progress" issue of my wine newsletter. I decided to stop by French Laundry, a pretty little stone-crafted restaurant where I had enjoyed several meals during the ownership of Don and Sally Schmitt. I'd heard there was a new owner, and as I walked around the property, I ran into a lanky, friendly guy at the back entrance to the kitchen. It was Tom Keller, and after we introduced ourselves, he suggested I stay for dinner, which I would have done were there not a commitment in San Francisco.

That was then, and now involves a reservation perhaps a couple months in advance. French Laundry has been lauded by some observers as the best restaurant in the world, which I believe is a bit over the top, but it is excellent by any standard. Moreover, Keller's New York establishment Per Se was one of four restaurants given three stars in Michelin's first New York City guide, and the only one with an American-born chef.

This is pretty impressive for someone who never took a formal cooking class. What has always struck me most about Keller, aside from his self-effacing demeanor, is his whimsicality in the kitchen.

# Corks & Forks

If you order the appetizer "Bacon and Eggs," for example, it's a poached quail egg topped with thinly sliced applewood-smoked bacon. "Oysters and Pearls" brings you a tapioca-sabayon gratin topped with plump oysters. Truffled *crème fraîche* accompanied by lengths of crusty russet potato goes under the name "Chips and Dip." There's "Tongue in Cheek," braised beef cheeks with slices of veal tongue on a horseradish cream. Keller's take on *pot au feu*, the French classic, involves braised beef short ribs, root vegetables, and sautéed marrow. "Coffee and Doughnuts" combines feather-light, cinnamon-dusted *beignets* comparable to the best of New Orleans with a *cappuccino semifreddo*. Simply masterly, all of it.

When I said Tom was not classically trained in the academic sense, it's important to note that he was not untrained. Before he purchased French Laundry in 1994, he had apprenticed at such noted Paris restaurants as Guy Savoy, Gérard Besson (a personal favorite) and Taillevent. When he came back to the United States, he opened the well reviewed Rakel in New York, and after five years there, he switched coasts to become executive chef at the trendy Checkers Hotel in Los Angeles.

I'm often asked how the restaurant got the name French Laundry. At one stage in its life, the building was just that, at others a personal residence, a brothel, and a saloon (not all at the same time). Today, in its country setting, it is the chicest of chic, as tough a reservation as there probably is in the country. Is it worth the effort? You bet it is, and be prepared for a four-hour experience, since Keller is famed for sending out bonus courses to frame what you've ordered from the menu. And the wines, as you'd expect, are superbly chosen.

I'm also asked how one person can manage two first-rank restaurants three thousand miles apart. Keller came up with an ingenious solution. He installed a wide-screen TV in the kitchen of Per Se in New York, a wide-angle lens focusing on the cooking line at French Laundry. When at Per Se, Keller monitors the screen while working, and if he sees something he doesn't like, he picks up a direct phone line.

Since French Laundry, Keller in conjunction with his brother opened a very satisfying bistro, Bouchon, at the southern end of Napa Valley, in Yountville. Now there's another Bouchon, which opened in 2004 at the Venetian in Las Vegas. It confounds me how Tom Keller can keep together these four projects, anchored by two world-class restaurants, but he does. He's a singular man.

## ⤙ MARK MILLER ⤚

Except for a trace of the accent, you'd never know Mark was from the Boston area, nor would you guess that from his food, which is solidly Southwestern.

I first met Mark, a voluble, energy-filled person, when he was doing important work in the kitchen at Chez Panisse. Later, he opened Fourth Street Grill in Berkeley, its emphasis on creatively prepared, fresh seasonal ingredients, paralleling what he had done at Chez Panisse. His Southwestern side came forth at his Santa Fe

Bar & Grill, also in Berkeley, which debuted in 1980. He eventually followed his heart and soul to Santa Fe, where he opened Coyote Café in 1987.

Now let's assume you are not exactly up to speed on Southwestern cuisine, which most Americans are not, and I was not on my first visit to Coyote Café, shortly after it opened. At Sante Fe Bar & Grill, Mark had put together an interesting mixture of Cajun, Creole, and Southwestern dishes, but at Coyote Café he's focused directly on the Southwest. That means chiles, a great variety of them, and as if to underscore the point, Miller wrote *The Great Chile Book*, with intelligent text and beautiful color illustrations, which combined, give you all you need to know about chiles.

In first visiting Coyote Café, I was particularly drawn to how Miller employed his beloved chiles, of course. Jalapenos figured importantly in a deep, earthy black bean soup; dried New Mexico red chiles and *anchos* enlivened Red Chile Pesto Clams; and Pork Loin with Cascabel Chile and Grapefruit Sauce was an unusual, remarkable Miller creation.

Something I didn't at first know about Mark was that his academic background at UC Berkeley concentrated on cultural anthropology and Chinese art history. The latter played a major part in his next venture, Loongbar in San Francisco's Ghirardelli Square. Not only did the restaurant quickly establish itself as the primary pan-Asian destination in San Francisco, but Mark's own art collection handsomely decorated the brick walls. Loongbar eventually morphed into another Asian-themed restaurant, and Miller is back at Coyote Café in Santa Fe, the place he loves best.

Mark is a man of diverse culinary talents, ranging from contemporary American to specifically Southwestern to pan-Asian. I can't think of anyone else who's bridged these gastronomic areas with such skill. Next time in Sante Fe or first time, you simply mustn't miss Coyote Café and the uniqueness of Mark Miller's cooking. In doing so, you'll discover contemporary and traditional Southwest cuisine within steps of Native American artisans who display their beautiful creations without even the slightest hint of the hard sell.

# 3

# Parsing Burgundy

## *Distinguishing Famous Vineyards from Gifted Winemakers*

*O*n *first making the short* twenty-five-mile drive from Beaune in the south to Dijon going north, you have traversed one of the most famed stretches of vineyards on earth, bucolic as can be, seeing the names of famous vineyards trip by every time you glance out the window over the beautifully sloping hills.

But if you're a wine professional, you're in pretty much a hornets' nest here. I quickly learned that there are levels within levels, boxes within boxes, both in the vineyards themselves and those who make wine from them.

The obvious first thing you must know about Burgundy is that there are only two grapes that really matter, Chardonnay and Pinot Noir. And if you think of those from a broad brush understanding of the varietal type, especially with a California perspective, you'll be wrong in Burgundy, because both grapes can reach their pinnacles of performance there and nowhere else, many on tiny parcels of land seemingly indistinguishable from the parcels alongside. That's the magic of Burgundy, the microcosm of *terroir*. Someone in Meursault may make four different wines from sites you can cast one long glance across without distinguishing one from another, but if the winemaking is true to the *terroirs*, they will be quite distinctive, one to another.

Using another perspective, assume you're standing on the Upper West Side of Manhattan, looking across Central Park to the East Side. Further assume that you're in a vineyard (fanciful, of course) and that you're looking across two others in the Park to a fourth on the other side of Fifth Avenue. Were you in Burgundy, say in Romanée-Conti, from the same vantage point as my hypothetical one in New York, you could easily be seeing through the Park and across it to the vineyards of Richebourg and Romanée-Saint-Vivant, the wines from each so very different one from the other, in their counterpoints of strength and finesse. That's Burgundy. Small squares, finely drawn.

A critical further point of knowledge for me in Burgundy was coming to know the different natures of those who live there and make the wine. Once you perceive that, you have a good chance of getting to the essence of what you have to know. Burgundian wine people can be either artisans or crass businesspersons, and you have to be careful in distinguishing among them, especially since they can be equally charming. Over time, I've roughed out three general but workable categorizations. Starting from the top, there is the Burgundian aristocracy, such as Domaine de la Romanée-Conti and Marquis d'Angerville; the established artisan producers such as Domaine Dujac; and the large commercial firms, among them Bouchard and Latour. The latter maintain tasting rooms in touristy Beaune, and they're fun to visit, if you have limited time in Burgundy.

When I first visited Romanée-Conti, I was astonished to see *interdit aux dames* as signage on the cellar door, an expression of an old Burgundian superstition that the natural flora of women will spoil wines still in barrel. I thought that odd especially since the codirector of Romanée-Conti at the time was Lalou Bize-Leroy, then as now a taster with a palate as fine as I have known. She received us, and the women in our party, signage notwithstanding, with Aubert de Villaine, now the managing partner of the estate, and with the legendary cellarmaster André Noblet.

Noblet, a gentle giant, came across to me immediately as someone who was so rooted in where he was that he was virtually speaking through the fruit he had so carefully nurtured. Montrachet I knew of course, but not at this level, pure Chardonnay, buttery and rich and yet so balanced, even young from barrel. Noblet was known with his broad Burgundian smile to describe his wines in feminine terms. "This Echézeaux," he commented, dipping from the barrel, "is Catherine Deneuve." And in rightly admiring his richer Romanée-Conti of the same year, he shrugged his shoulders and said simply "Sophia Loren."

At Romanée-Conti, I set my benchmark. I learned what Pinot

Noir was at its best, and how others should be evaluated. I also caught Lalou Bize-Leroy's attention by observing off-handedly that perhaps the human factor, brilliance in grape growing and winemaking, transcended the character of the *terroir* itself. "Nothing could be farther from the truth!" she said. "And let me construct a tasting for you next time you're here to prove my point." I made a mental note to take her up on that.

But at the moment I was on my way to see Jean Gros, also in Vosne, who showed me a brilliant Vosne-Romanée "Clos des Réas" as well as several other barrel samples, without exception of top quality. Gros was the quintessential gruff Burgundian, not so used to foreign visitors, wise quickly to those whom he thought understanding of his craft, and warm as could be from then on. When he showed me the best that had been marketed in the United States, it was a disappointment. When I told him, with a wry smile, he said, "What you tasted here was not exported." When I arrived at my hotel, I discovered a case of the top-shelf stuff in the trunk of my car.

There could have been no more different a personality than Jacques Seysses at Domaine Dujac in Morey-Saint-Denis. Recently established there when I first visited, Jacques, son of a French food magnate and representative of a new generation, had begun making some of the clearest, most compelling Pinots I had yet tasted. He was even brave enough to show me some of his '68s, a horrible year in which to have started, but still made as well as possible and quite drinkable in youth. So clear was the definition of his better wines that they created a particularly accurate declination of the territory.

As always in Burgundy, you set your footing in the basic wine and expand from there. At Dujac, the base is Morey-Saint-Denis *tout court* as they say, or the straight-out appellation, which expresses itself with light but defined Pinot fruit and oak just in the right partnership with it. A little west, less than a half mile from the village but importantly up a slope favored by sun late in the day, are the *grands crus* Clos Saint Denis and Clos de la Roche, the latter my favorite for its expression of fruit, greater concentration of berry character, by just a bit, than I found in the Clos Saint Denis. Best of all was the Bonnes-Mares just over the border into Chambolle, somehow just that much richer and more important than these other excellent Pinots. But each of these expressed exactly where they came from. It made me think again of what Lalou Bize-Leroy had emphasized about *terroir*.

So I took her up on her challenge and set a date for what she titled *Quelques Terroirs de Gevrey Chambertin, 1959–1977*. I thought it would be a morning tasting, but was I ever wrong. Mme. Bize-Leroy had selected forty wines, which took us all day to assess, with a brief break for a simple lunch and mineral water. I framed my tasting notes, and they adorn my office today. I concluded that Lalou was in essence correct, in that Gevrey "Les Champeaux" was distinctly lighter than the obviously muscular "Les Cazetiers," the Charmes-Chambertin and Le Chambertin bringing the whole Gevrey idea together in marvelous harmony of grace and power, much in the way Beethoven's First and Ninth Symphonies are relatives, the latter simply grander. But of course Mme. Bize-Leroy was selecting, and the wines came from vineyards that had been exemplary to her for years.

On reflection, I thought it might be a good idea to return from exceptional wines and intricate analysis to something simpler. I thought first about what Aubert de Villaine and his wife were producing at their estate in Bouzeron, at the southern end of Burgundy proper, quite apart in distance and concept from Romanée-Conti. Bouzeron is one of the prettiest hamlets in this part of Burgundy, with nothing to draw the day-tripper tourist except the nearby restaurant Lameloise, but with everything to draw someone who wants to experience the beauty of a southern Burgundy village unimpaired by time.

These wines are bottled as A. & P. de Villaine, the "P" being Aubert's American wife, Pamela. What I saw in tasting with the gently scholarly Aubert was purity of varietal character, straight out. Their Aligoté, a local grape lower in reputation than Chardonnay but beloved in the region, was excellent by being straight and simple, brightly fruity and edged just enough with acid. The same was true with their Chardonnay "Les Clous," not the richer product typical of great vineyards to the north, but a perfectly formed lighter Burgundy with appealing pear tones, and so much more appealing than most of the commercial Mâcons nearby. So it went with their "La Digoine" Pinot Noir, light, silky, gracious, expressively varietal with its berry fruit.

# Corks & Forks

There is also a pretty amusing connection between the Seysses and the de Villaines. Rosalyn Seysses and Pamela de Villaine were close school friends in northern California when they both had the lark of an idea of being pickers for a harvest in Burgundy. So they did, and subsequently, Rosalyn married Jacques, Pamela married Aubert, and even though that might seem a silly Italian opera plot, it has resulted in much happiness for four exceptional people.

Through Aubert de Villaine, I met Rebecca Wasserman. Begin by understanding that the wine business in Burgundy has historically been principally a men's club. Recall what I said about Romanée-Conti posting a sign saying that women were not allowed in the cellars, even though one of the ownership group then was a woman. So enter Ms. Wasserman, an American who came to Burgundy because her husband, a painter, favored the light there.

Slim to none would have seemed her chances to establish a business to represent established and emerging vintners for sales to the United States. A woman? And an American woman at that? But as we went from property to property, from tasting the mineraly, classic Meursaults of Francois Jobard to the silky and forthcoming Pinots of Simon Bize in Becky's home village of Savigny-les-Beaune, and many others, I saw respect, which does not come easily in Burgundy, extended to us both, something you learn to perceive here in the flick of an eye or perhaps a sly smile as you and the vintner taste together. Unless you know a vintner already, he is trying you out, and he will make his own judgment quite quickly on your reaction to the samples he offers. You can only imagine the trust, the leap of faith, implicit in allowing an American woman to represent your treasured wines in a U.S. market known by you, the vintner, not well, or not at all. That's what Becky was doing when first I met her, and it's what she's continued to succeed in doing ever since.

But Burgundy remains a conundrum to any non-Burgundian. It can be welcoming, or not. Its wines can be honestly presented, or chosen from best barrels to make the best impression. But the best examples are supernal, far overshadowing the mediocrities —which is why the finest Burgundies are so often compared to the most memorable affairs of the heart.

# 4

# Popping the Cork
# in Champagne

*f you've visited other* wine districts in France before landing
in Champagne, which is quite likely, you'll be struck by several salient things. First, it's small, only 60,000 acres in contrast to roughly 2,250,000 under vine in France overall. Second,
unlike Bordeaux and Burgundy, which comprise numerous wine
villages, Champagne revolves around two small cities, Reims and
Epernay. Third, like Bordeaux but unlike any other French wine
district, Champagne in the wine sense is about as English as it is
French. Furthermore, there is a huge disparity between the scale
of the vast international houses and the small producers, remind-
ing me of how in Napa Valley a tiny winery can be within shouting
distance of Robert Mondavi.

Reims and Epernay would be pretty undistinguished French
provincial towns but for the magnificent fourteenth-century
Gothic cathedral in Reims and for the wine, apparently developed
by the eighteenth-century Benedictine monk Dom Pérignon, who
is credited with transforming the region's traditional lightly sparkling wine into what we now know as Champagne.

# Popping the Cork in Champagne

First, as a tourist, I did what anyone would do and visited the major houses, saw the endless cellars and the thousands of bottles slumbering away, watched the process of *dégorgement* in which the plug of yeast sediment is expelled from the neck of the bottle then made ready for market. Later, as a critic, I learned much more about the inner workings of the region.

Although the *grandes maisons* dominate by architectural prominence and reputation, very few control the majority of the vineyards producing the grapes for their wines. They depend on local growers, most smaller than larger, so that while Champagne from a touristic viewpoint is elegant, the base is solidly agrarian. On any tour at a major house, you will be received well indeed, although I've found the tours formulaic. As for the tunneled cellars, to apply Ronald Reagan's unfortunately chosen observation on California's redwoods, it is true here that if you've seen one, you've seen them all.

I quickly came to understand that perceiving Champagne, beyond the superficial, required a focus. I decided to concentrate on medium-size producers of top quality and small grower-producers making their individual statements. Based on tasting experience, I centered on Pol Roger in the first category, then among the smaller houses I chose Billecart-Salmon and Albert Lassalle.

It has been since 1849 that Pol Roger has been producing superb Champagne, from a background in the first-rate district of Ay. The wines are full-flavored but elegant, highlighted for me by "Cuvée Sir Winston Churchill," who favored Pol Roger all his life and asked, as legend has it, that a magnum be delivered to his bath each morning. Pol Roger returned the favor by naming its prestige bottling for him.

I met Christian Pol Roger, whose blond good looks seem more Dutch than French, early in my writing career. For some years, he had been directing the company in conjunction with his cousin Christian de Billy. He received me in his elegantly understated office and study, and then came a major surprise—the 1921 Pol Roger.

It's often said that Champagne doesn't age well, losing brightness and taking on a nutty character that some like and some don't. In my experience, older Champagnes from fine years, if well stored, remain amazingly fresh. That was the case with this 1921, its color still rather youthful if slightly going to gold, its fruit still present, its bubbles soft and gentle. I've never had a disappointing bottle from Pol Roger, but that 1921 eclipses them all.

I'd give comparable praise to Billecart-Salmon in Mareuil-sur-Ay, a suburb of a small town (you could blink and have driven through Ay), but that's how this part of France is laid out. I first discovered this great family-owned producer (since 1818) in San Francisco, following up later on its own turf. Not a great deal of wine is produced, but I keep going back to the Brut with that magic combination of flavor and elegance, and to the Brut Rosé, forward with fine red-fruit character but none of the sweetness some associate with pink sparklers.

In exploring Champagne, I decided to visit Lassalle, about

six miles south of Reims in Chigny-les-Roses, a small producer whose remarkable wines were (and are) represented by my local importer-retailer friend Kermit Lynch. It took me lots of wrong twists and turns to find Lassalle, on what should have been a short drive as the crow flies, but in this part of Champagne that's not how it works if you're on four wheels rather than two wings. But once at Lassalle, the reception and the wines were equally exceptional. What you look for from this fine family house are the crisp, lightly fruity Cachet d'Or and the richer Impérial Préférence.

There are few shortcuts or easy answers in the pricey Champagne world. I've offered some recommendations, to which I'd add without the above detail Veuve Clicquot Yellow Label and N/V Charles Heidsieck, both for consistent flavor quality and value. You can go over the moon, if you choose, with Dom Pérignon or Cristal, but if this be your playing field, it has to be Krug, plain and simple.

Here's a tip you might want to keep in mind in scouting out Champagne, one I learned early on and which has proved useful over the years. It has to do with the small print on the lower part of the labels. "NM" (*negociant-manipulant*) indicates that the bottler has brought in some grapes or wine to blend with its own, a common practice among the larger houses, whereas "RM" (*récoltant-manipulant*) identifies wine made from the vintner's own grapes. "MA" (*marque d'acheteur*) is the one to be careful with, since it indicates bought-in wine, private-labeled and destined for the mass market at the low price it mostly deserves.

# Corks & Forks

You'll note I haven't referred to American "champagnes," since they are not Champagne, and most of the best American producers, such as Domaine Carneros, Domaine Chandon, and Roederer Estate do not use the word on their labels. That's in part related to their French partnerships, but also because they understand that Champagne is Champagne, pure and simple, and its best, pure and sublime.

Much has been written about whether Champagne does or doesn't go well with food, and over the years, I've concluded that it really does not, except in specific situations. Champagne is meant to be an apéritif with or without appropriate companions such as mildly flavored hors d'oeuvres or oysters. With more robust fare, most Champagnes don't have enough there there, to quote Gertrude Stein from another context.

### ⌐ CLAUDE TAITTINGER ⌐

Claude Taittinger epitomizes the region and the concept, for both accomplishment and elegance. When we arrived at Reims by train from Paris, Claude was there to greet us himself and promptly whisked us off to his home for lunch. First we chatted over Champagne, overlooking his lovely garden, and in the course of conversation it turned out that we shared a fetish—London shirts. We agreed: They aren't quite right until after the second laundering.

This venerable estate, established in 1743, came under full control of the Taittinger family in 1933. Since Claude took control

# Popping the Cork in Champagne

in 1960—his nephew Pierre-Emmanuel subsequently at his side—concentration has been all about maintenance of the house style, that about finesse, exemplified by predominance of Chardonnay in the blends and exclusivity in the flagship Comtes de Champagne, its vineyard history dating from the nineth or eleventh century, depending on how you parse, but anyway, a long time. The wine, as Claude explained, has not achieved the international renown associated with Dom Pérignon and Cristal, beloved of rock and film celebrities, because, first of all, there isn't very much of it. And promoting it to that crowd is surely not his style.

Taittinger also produces an utterly stunning Comtes de Champagne Rosé, belying the myth that pink Champagne is frivolous. This one is surely not, the Pinot fruit occupying center stage in a dry environment, and despite what I've said about Champagne with food, this one would be perfect with the likes of pink duck breast or pork tenderloin. And I believe that Claude, ever the gentleman, would join me in raising a flute to that idea.

## ⤞ RÉMY KRUG ⤝

When I first met Rémy, a contemporary in age, while tasting samples together in the family's cellars in Reims, I realized I was under scrutiny. As we exchanged opinions on what we were evaluating, he spontaneously invited me for lunch at Boyer, the Michelin three-star nearby. I must have passed muster.

Over lunch, which began with a spectacular 1962, Rémy explained what makes Krug so special. Dating from the 1860s, the firm has consistently been in family hands. Grapes are selected from the best vineyards, and they are fermented in small oak, Krug and Bollinger being among the few still taking that approach. The Grand Cuvée, the most frequently seen Krug, may have up to ten vintage components, thus its depth and complexity. It may typically have up to seven years' yeast contact in the bottle before *dégorgement*.

The Krug family bought and replanted roughly five acres in Le Mesnil in 1971, and the first release of the 1979 Clos du Mesnil, as Rémy explained, was an experiment with 100 percent Chardonnay. It's a bit of a departure from typical style for Krug, but a brilliant wine with a price to match.

# 5

# How I Found Prime Italian Vineyards with a New Zealand Race Car Driver

*ike most of us,* you probably grew up thinking of Italian wine as dismal Chianti in straw-covered flasks and tasteless so-called Soaves poured by the glass. When I started writing about wine, I found that many of the Italians I liked bore the name Neil Empson on the back label as exporter, and I devoted part of one of my newsletters to descriptions of several of them. Empson was in touch, and said he would soon be in San Francisco. We made a plan to have lunch at what was at the time my favorite Italian restaurant.

When I met Neil, I thought here is David Niven in his prime, both in looks and wit. He explained that after his Formula One experiment in New Zealand, he moved to New York, became involved in restaurant management, and met his Italian American wife, Maria. After increasing appreciation of Italian wine, in part related to visits to Italian vineyards, Neil made his decision. He announced to Maria that they were moving to Italy to pursue the selection and export of top-quality wines. At the conclusion of our lunch, he suggested that we meet in Milan for a tour among his producers. Since I had an upcoming Italy trip already on the books, I was able to take him up on his invitation sooner rather than later.

Empson had chosen to concentrate his business on the whites of the north, Collio and Tre Venezie, and reds from Tuscany and Piemonte. Navigating this part of Italy is not difficult or time-consuming, especially with Neil at the wheel of his major Mercedes.

Our first stop leaving Milan was to be Pieropan in Soave. I knew the wines and considered them among the best of the region. On the way, Empson said "Here's what's going to happen. The old man will be napping, and his wife will try to up the price for this vintage." We arrive at the rustic estate with an elderly gentleman snoozing in his chair, as predicted, and his wife saying to Neil, "has to be a higher price this year." Neil responded by kissing her hand and saying *sempre più giovene* (ever younger), at which she shrugs and says, "I guess we can keep it the same, for friendship."

Up north, almost to the former Yugoslavia, we visit Jermann, the scholarly demeanor of Silvio perhaps reflected in the complexity of his Vintage Tunina, made from a careful blend of Chardonnay, Ribolla, Malvasia, and Picolit. That specialty is worth asking for wherever you can find it, or for that matter any of the Jermann whites. Neil warned me that nearby Mario Schiopetto was

a quirky fellow making superb Pinot Bianco and Tocai, also a grace-
ful Merlot-based red blend. Schiopetto, though a friend of Empson, was indeed quirky, putting out our tasting samples, including
the whites, at room temperature from previously opened bottles.
After a brief stop at Vittorio Puiatti's EnoFriulia and enjoyment of
his fresh, un-oaked whites, we were off to red-wine country.

We made a stop at Monte Vertine, Radda in Chianti as the district is called, guests of Sergio Manetti, industrialist turned wine
producer. He had kindly invited us for dinner and to spend the
night. Of course, we tasted the wines first, highlighted by his 100
percent Sangiovese Le Pergole Torte, followed by a sequence
of his Chianti Classico *riservas*. At dinner, we enjoyed the best
rosemary-seasoned birds I've ever had, as well as the company of
his two lovely daughters, I'd guess in their early twenties. After a
few sips of grappa, Neil and I were off to our rooms.

There was a rap on my door at 6:00 A.M., and when I opened
it, there was Sergio. "How did you sleep?" he said, to which I
responded, "I *was* sleeping very well." A little later we all had
a simple breakfast, after which Neil and I set off for Piemonte.
Once in the car Neil, mastering the curves, asked, "Did Sergio
knock on your door this morning?" When I said yes, with a chuckle
he responded, "He knocked on mine too. He was checking on
the girls."

As Sangiovese is the principal red grape in Tuscany, Nebbiolo is the major player in Piemonte, expressing itself most
profoundly in Barbaresco and Barolo. It can show characteristics

of Pinot Noir, to which it is apparently related, making it seem like Beaune-style Burgundy in some hands, a much denser red as made by others. Angelo Gaja surely falls into that category with such single-vineyard bottlings as Sorì San Lorenzo, Sorì Tildin, and Costa Russi. These are as dense as Nebbiolo gets in Piemonte, but Gaja lightens up a bit with Vinot, similar to the more serious Beaujolais.

We connected again with Gaja, a stocky and utterly charming man, at *Ristorante da Guido* in Costigliole d'Asti, one of the smallest but brightest Piedmont stars of the time. The evening was particularly unusual for Guido Alciati's willingness to open on a closed night for our small group, but he was paying respects to Angelo Gaja for many reasons, among them his representation of the Burgundian wines of Domaine de la Romanée-Conti, which Alciati adored and served forth with pride and pleasure that evening. His wife, Lidia, the chef, did wondrous things with local seasonal game, right on point with the wines.

This was my introduction to the truffle gatherers called *trifiolau*, locals who employ their dogs to find and sniff out the precious objects. They generally do business at the back door of the restaurant, and honestly. The highly prized truffles are priced by weight, and Alciati showed us one having been filled with buckshot, the flesh, as recipes say, reserved for another use.

We could have gone on to other estates, many of which we both knew already, but with pedal to the metal, Empson sped us back to Milan. It had been a great experience.

# How I Found Prime Italian Vineyards

## ⌐ MARCHESE PIERO ANTINORI ⌐

You might assume that if your family has been making wine in Tuscany since the fourteenth century, that you occupy the upper floors of the Palazzo Antinori at Piazza Antinori in central Florence, and if you trust my wife that you're the sexiest Italian man imaginable, you might be hard to know.

Not so Piero. Nor his beautiful wife or his three daughters, all their first names beginning with "A," and all involved one way or another in the family business. Having met Piero first in the United States, I called him spontaneously after a Florentine lunch. His assistant put me right through. "Bob, you're in Florence. Great news! Any chance you could come over now? I'm playing with a sparkling wine, and I'd like your opinion." Piero received me at the Palazzo as casually dressed as I was, and though we both liked the wine, we shook our heads negatively with regard to the likely U.S. market for it.

Some few years later, Piero and I were in more serious discussion with his senior winemaking advisor, the redoubtable Dottore Giacomo Tachis, one of the most esteemed wine professionals in Italy. The question at issue was what to do about maintaining the Chianti Classico DOCG (*Denominazione di origine controllata e garantita*) labeling for Antinori's principal reds. The rules for making Chianti Classico were set forth by the Barone Ricasoli in the mid-nineteenth century, in an effort to legitimatize an often debased wine, but they included a 20 percent proportion of white grapes as a benefit to growers of such grapes who had no other home for them, and as an attempt to soften what was then frequently a rough product. Piero and Dr. Tachis always believed that the best wines of the region should be 100 percent red, and our tastings surely confirmed that. They had broken out first with the very lovely 1971 Tignanello, a blend of Sangiovese and Canaiolo, later to become Sangiovese and Cabernet Sauvignon, a stunning nontraditional Chianti blend.

In 2004, Piero took the very major step of changing the composition of the firm's landmark Villa Antinori Chianti Classico from the DOCG stipulated blend to all red, including nontraditional varieties together with Sangiovese, that meaning declassification from DOCG Chianti Classico to the lesser IGT, or *Indicazione di Geographica Tipica*. Piero's decision was based on his belief that Villa Antinori was more reflective of its territorial history than of bureaucratic rulemaking, including grape stipulation, and current releases prove him correct. The wine simply stands on its own.

So did Piero, on one memorable evening at Buca di Lappi, the starkly bright trattoria below ground at the palazzo, around the corner from the admirable Cantinetta Antinori. We were perhaps eight, Piero to my right. He had brought some intriguing older Antinori reds from upstairs, and with a gentle touch on my arm, he said, "Just let me order, OK?" Doing so brought first a small plate of pasta as light as air, and next the main event, *Bistecca alla Fiorentina*, which has nothing to do with the simply grilled large sirloin that travels under that name in America or, for practical purposes, anywhere outside Tuscany. The key is the beef, from those lazy Chianchina whitish animals that you see while traversing Tuscany. The meat is midway between veal and beef in color, a bit more highly flavored than veal, in sum unique.

A server bought tableside a marble-topped trolley with a full loin for Piero's inspection, and in sotto voce conversation they decided exactly which sections should be cut. In short order, here came slices of the very finest *Bistecca alla Fiorentina* I had ever had or ever expect to have, the meat grilled rare and juicy, scattered with mild herbs, drizzled with the finest olive oil, of course produced by Antinori. White beans of the region were the perfect partners. And of course were the well aged Chianti Classicos Piero had chosen.

As he always has, Piero will continue to chart his own course through the thicket of Tuscan regulation, always with the intent of making the very best and most typical wines from his nine vineyard properties, each with a personality as distinctive as his own.

## ⌁ BURTON ANDERSON ⌁

On paper, Anderson might not seem a candidate to be one of the world's prime authorities on Italian wine, which he is. Born in Minneapolis (don't forget Robert Mondavi grew up in Minnesota), he obtained a journalism degree at the University of Minnesota and almost immediately moved to Europe, where in fairly short order he became a chief editor on the *International Herald Tribune*. Along the way he developed a passion for Italian wine, expressed in part by his purchasing a beautiful little wine-growing estate on the fringes of Chianti, on hillside land near Florence.

After first meeting Burton in the United States, he kindly asked me to be a houseguest next time in Tuscany, and I readily took him up on that. Visiting the smaller wineries and local *trattorie* with Burton I found comparable going to a baseball game with a college friend who became a professional pitcher. In both instances, I was pointed to nuances I might not have picked up on my own, and in Anderson's case small restaurants I most likely would never have found.

His first book, *Vino*, I consider quite the best survey of Italian wine and winemakers in English, but sadly it is out of print, though you can find the random copy on Amazon.com. More magnificent, in part because of its regional maps and gorgeous photographs, is *Wine Atlas of Italy*, never out of my car when traversing Italian vineyard territory, which can be challenging. Moreover, Anderson offers in this book tips on where to visit and taste, region by region, and I've never been disappointed by one of his recommendations.

Most recently he's produced *Treasures of the Italian Table*, an intelligent and concisely written examination of such Italian culinary stars as *Tartuffi Bianchi d'Alba, Olio Extra Virgine, Parmigiano Romano,* and *Risotto.* It's not a recipe book, but a great read from a man who has happily adopted another country, and judging from my experiences with him there, a country that has embraced him just as warmly.

And what could not be liked about someone who named a child Gaia, just as Burton's close friend Angelo Gaja in Piemonte did with one of his children?

### ⌁ LEONARDO LOCASIO ⌁

Leonardo and I met over lunch, an invitation that, as a critic, I routinely turn down from wine importers. But I had been attracted by several bottlings bearing his name, in large part because they came from districts in Italy as yet very little known in the United States. Accepting that lunch invitation turned out to be a wise decision.

He brought several interesting wines, mostly from southern Italy, but much more interesting to me was the man himself, Italian-born but with an American education, including an MBA from the University of Chicago followed by a time of management consulting with the estimable McKinsey & Co. Since that background pretty much paralleled my own (except for being born Italian), we spent the first part of lunch trading consulting war stories and then focused on Leonardo's business plan, which was in essence his MBA graduation paper.

He thought, quite correctly, that even in the '80s Americans still thought of Italian wines as cheap Chiantis (remember those straw-covered flasks?) and dreadful whites traveling under the name Soave. His idea, given the burgeoning American interest in wine, was to bring forward quality Italian wines not yet seen here, principally from outside the familiar regions of Piedmont and Tuscany. He knew it was at the time a niche market, but he also saw it as a growth market.

And how right he was. LoCasio's company, Winebow, now represents seventy-odd Italian producers from the venerable such as Anselmi (real Soave!), Maculan, and Schiopetto up north, to equally distinguished names from the south, among them Taurino in Apulia, and Tasca in Sicily. Think whites from the north, reds from the south.

What LoCasio saw so presciently was a conjunction of American interest in good wine at a fair price, finer wine at a higher notch, and Italy's ability to provide both. Thus the success of Winebow, and the reliability of the "Leonardo LoCasio Selection" on any of its bottles.

# 6

# Seeking the Unusual
# in Dining

*oo many people* seeking memorable dining experiences fall
into the trap of focusing on famed places with their difficult
reservations, often diffident service, and unpredictable food.
Here's my short list of advice.

* For the most part, stay away from the most famed places, especially in large cities, where you have a better-than-average
chance of being under-served and over-charged.

* If you're in France and using Michelin, avoid at all costs the
three-stars, and those are substantial costs. Troisgros and
Guérard would be significant exceptions.

* You should focus on the one-stars or on those with two or three
crossed forks.

* Focus intensely on what the city does best and concentrate
on that, asking advice as necessary, preferably from your hotel
concierge, most of whom are very well informed. For example,
a good concierge in San Francisco would never send you to

touristy Fishermen's Wharf for the city's famed seafood, but rather to one of several excellent downtown restaurants.

◄ Buy the local city magazine or events periodical, which often have detailed restaurant listings. And on the same thought, pay attention to *Gourmet* and *Bon Appétit*, the restaurant coverage in both well worth attention. It was from reading *Gourmet* that I discovered Peter Langan and Odin's.

◄ Make extensive use of random conversation with locals. Very often over a latte or a glass of wine, you can glean just the restaurant information you need, no books required. This approach has surely worked for me.

### ⌐ MICHEL GUÉRARD ⌐

If you live in Boston, you probably know, or know of, Dorchester and Mattapan. If you live in New York, you know that the area around Yankee Stadium in the Bronx is not where you want to be at night. If you know London, you also know the East End is not the best end.

That brings us to Asnières, a dismal and vaguely threatening community in a suburb of Paris, where I went to investigate the cooking of young chef Michel Guérard, whose contemporary approach to classic French cooking was raising eyebrows all over the gastronomic world. The best way of locating Guérard's restaurant was to point toward the brightest lights on the quiet, small main street.

And the place was a mini-riot of pleasure, obviously discovered by a legion of well-dressed Parisians. What struck me most was the intensity of the sauces, butter-free and composed from vegetable reductions. The absence of butter and cream was hardly missed, even with amply favored poultry and lamb. Guérard's approach to lightening the substance but not the flavors of sauces, and his emphasis on fresh, regional ingredients, became a principal part of the base of what came to be called nouvelle cuisine.

A few years later I met up with Michel at his sumptuous Les Prés d'Eugénie, near Pau in the southwest of France, a gorgeous property with twenty-two rooms and six suites, inherited by Guérard's wife. You aren't exactly in the middle of nowhere here, but you almost are, and if you're inclined to go, you should plan on dining (three Michelin stars), reading, and hiking if you're so oriented.

One night I was reading alone in the common room, after an uncommonly fine dinner, and suddenly the front door burst open, admitting the man himself. After we exchanged pleasantries, I asked Michel how he made the fantastic *marmalade d'oignons* which had accompanied the lamb I had so enjoyed at dinner. "If you have a few minutes, let's go in the kitchen and I'll show you," he said. For a while we were happily simmering a mass of thinly sliced onions with a little red wine, a little vinegar, a little sugar. But the aromas wafted up the stairs, and we heard "*Michel, ou es tu?*" and from my side of the house, "Robert, where are you?" It was probably 1:00 A.M.. Michel and I shared a Gallic shrug as we continued to finish our onions amidst the duet.

So many chefs, in France and worldwide, have been inspired by this self-effacing man's efforts to reduce fats while enhancing flavors, and he deserves multiple stars even beyond the red covers of Michelin.

### ⌐ PETER LANGAN ⌐

Where does one even start with Peter, one of the brilliant chefs I've ever known, but also one of the most self-destructive personalities I've known, too clearly demonstrated by his dying at an early age by tipping over a kerosene stove in his London home.

That implies drink, and that's right. Peter claimed to plough through a case of Champagne daily, and in awe, I saw him do a good part of that.

I met Langan quite innocently by following on a *Gourmet* article featuring London restaurants open late, and that's how I found Odin's, named in honor of a Danish lady friend of Langan, the restaurant still alive and well in Mayfair. My first meal there was so special, a branch of nouvelle cuisine London was barely seeing, I asked if I could speak with the chef, which was easily arranged, and thus began a long acquaintance.

Though Langan loved the cozy and upscale Odin's, where when not cooking he would frequently be seated with his wife and the aptly named dog Scrounge, he yearned for a London edition of the Paris landmark La Coupole, less formal and lots of fun.

Langan's Brasserie opened in 1976, diagonally across Piccadilly from the Ritz. I was there for the debut, but I couldn't believe what I saw in walking to the door.

Langan had acquired the premises of a '30s-style French restaurant, Le Coq d'Or, attracted by its space and ceiling heights, immense for London at the time (pre-Conran). When we had walked through the restaurant the evening before opening, I commented that the kitchen was the filthiest I had ever seen, and that keeping the out-of-style velvet banquettes in deep cherry was out of harmony with the cheery dining room, festooned with superb contemporary art, much of it by Peter's friend David Hockney. Langan ordered me off the premises, in no uncertain terms.

When I arrived the next evening, in pouring rain, I noticed a huge pile of drenched cherry banquettes on the sidewalk. No comment offered by Langan, or needed.

On a subsequent visit to Langan's Brasserie, under which name it continues to flourish, my wife and I were seated with Peter, chef (and now owner) Richard Shepherd, silent partner Michael Caine, Dudley Moore, and his lady friend of the time. For whatever reason, Langan went out of his way to be insulting to my wife, as was Moore to his friend, who left in tears. Another night at Langan's.

Several months later I had a first appointment with Rémy Krug, one of the greatest gentlemen of Champagne, a society which I have always considered more comparable to an association of London clubmen than to one of French vintners. At the cellars,

# Corks&Forks

M. Krug and I tasted through a number of still wines, which in various combination would become the next Krug blend. Spontaneously, Rémy invited me for lunch, at the three-star Boyer not far away. As we looked over the room of sleek diners, glasses of magnificent '62 Krug in hand, I noticed Langan at a hapless table of attending editors from *Harper's Queen* and the *London Times*, publications to which he occasionally contributed.

Then it happened. "Hey, Krug," Langan bellowed. "Having lunch with Finigan, are you?" The room went silent. The magazine people squirmed. I was appalled, but what to say to a man I'd barely met?

Rémy Krug admirably handled the situation when Langan, without invitation, came to our table and swigged from a decanter of a lovely Léoville-Las-Cases, dribbling a good deal down his white-suited front. Rémy fixed him with a steely gaze, and in a phrase from Victoriana, said "Peter, we are not amused."

Naturally, Peter found his way to San Francisco, where he loved the food and always wore his signature white suit, but he was unusually careful once in asking where he shouldn't walk late at night. I told him, but I might have known he would prowl exactly where I advised him not to. So he did, and was stabbed, but with good fortune not seriously.

It was the stove at home that did him in. A great talent, beset by personal demons, much admired by many and missed for himself at his best.

# Seeking the Unusual in Dining

## ∞ JEAN TROISGROS ∞

When I first met Jean, it was at the home of Mme. Lalou Bize-Leroy of Domaine Leroy, such a continuing formidably charming and talented presence in the rarified world of Burgundy. Each autumn she hosts a sort of salon at her home in Auxey-Duresses just north of Meursault to entertain a few respected friends for enjoyment of superb Burgundy, mostly Leroy of course, partnered with classic Burgundian dishes.

Lalou has a little parlor trick with which her regular guests were familiar, but with which I was not, on first visit, that being to begin the evening with blind tasting of a red she knows almost no one will be able to identify, even in this sort of company. This evening's mystery wine was something I thought of as a minor Burgundy from a lesser year in the '50s, but Troisgros was the first to speak. "I think it's a '57 Beaujolais," he said, "probably Moulin-à-Vent." A stunned Lalou exclaimed, *"Jean! Exactemente! Incroyable!"*

Keep in mind that most Beaujolais, meant to be drunk young, are dead when nearing their thirtieth birthday. But not this one. So in my first conversation with Jean Troisgros, whose mastery in the kitchen never did extend to English, he said with a grin and a little shoulder punch, "How did you guess it was from a poor year in the '50s? Want to join me at a few small cellars in the morning?"

Of course I did. We visited a few stunningly fine properties, so small I probably wouldn't have discovered them on my own, and over a simple lunch he said, "Have you been to our restaurant?" I said that I had, but not recently. "Well, call me when you can, and we can play some tennis, too, if you'd enjoy that."

I took him up on both counts. Now keep in mind that Troisgros in Roanne is not by far the image of the Paris three-star, but neither is Roanne comparable to Paris. It's a somewhat gritty city, in which Jean-Baptiste Troisgros established his bistro opposite the rail station in 1930. Surely he wouldn't have imagined that not so many years later his sons Jean and Pierre would have transformed his bistro into a Michelin three-star restaurant, with elegant rooms above, while maintaining the café section in front as a hangout for locals, who happily take their morning coffees there. But Jean and his brother Pierre had experience from age fifteen, in the French apprenticeship tradition, at such restaurants as Lucas-Carton in Paris and at La Pyramide in Vienne, there under the tutelage of the legendary Fernand Point.

Jean made it possible for me to experience all the aspects of Troisgros. When I called to fulfill his invitation to visit, we were in Bordeaux, and I miscalculated the driving time to Roanne, which is roughly a 350-mile trip over twisty roads, in this instance complicated by a driving rainstorm. When I realized we would never make our Saturday reservation time, I called ahead, and after a pause the receptionist said, "The kitchen will be closed, but M. Troisgros says you will not go hungry, and you are welcome for lunch tomorrow in place of dinner tonight."

Not going hungry meant silky slabs of the finest foie gras, the best bread, and a memorable bottle of Champagne from Jean's own stock, all erasing and then some the torture of the drive, and this at a beautifully set table in that front area where the regulars have their cafés in the morning. Perfection, as was the spacious and well-fitted-out room Jean had chosen for these two tired bodies, just a welcome few steps up from the restaurant.

We had been slotted in for a one o'clock lunch Sunday, and with great good fortune Jean had chosen to seat us at his private table in an alcove within the large kitchen. You've probably read horror stories about kitchen histrionics, how chefs scream at their assistants and especially at the apprentices. In contrast, watching everyone work in the airy, bright, modern Troisgros kitchen was like being at a ballet, except for the soft murmur of conversation across stations. Jean was both cooking and supervising, occasionally pointing a finger here, offering a comment there, his eyes everywhere including on what he was preparing himself.

Our lunch was highlighted by a perfectly sautéed filet of salmon wrapped, incredibly, in a latticework of yellow and green pasta, on a mustard-tinged white wine reduction. While we were exulting in the fish, Jean was gently braising rabbit loins in a soft, complex red wine sauce, perfect in itself and even better with the Gevrey-Chambertin he chose. After lunch, Jean said, "I'm going over to Burgundy tomorrow and staying at Lalou's daughter's house. Maybe we could make lunch there."

Make lunch with Jean Troisgros? Well, why not. In the late morning, he foraged with my wife and a few other visitors for root vegetables in the garden behind the house. What he had in mind was a country-style ragout of the vegetables with local sausage, so while the vegetable team was doing its work, under his direction, Jean suggested that he and I visit his favorite local butcher. There must have been twenty choices, but Troisgros eyed exactly the sausages he wanted, and back we were in the kitchen in no time.

He directed the prepping of the vegetables, while he sliced and sautéed the sausages. Heaping the vegetables into a pot, he said to me, "Put in a bottle of white wine and reduce." While Jean was working with the sausages, I was apparently being too gentle with the vegetables, as I learned abruptly when he looked over, raised my heat by double, and barked "I said reduce, not simmer!" It was a great lunch.

Then there was the tennis. Jean was passionate about the game, and he was physically right for it, lean and agile. But he was more than ten years my senior, and I had no doubt I could outmatch him, even playing on clay, more his surface than mine. But I've always noted that wily tennis players don't worry if you win a few games early on because they're looking for weaknesses to exploit later on, and that's just what Jean did with me. Over the course of several matches, I never did prevail, and I was especially saddened, some years later, to learn that Jean's sudden death was caused by a heart malady on the court.

I found Jean Troisgros one of the greatest chefs and wine tasters of my experience, a witty and generous man—and one hell of a tennis player.

*Seeking the Unusual in Dining*

## ⇒ TRADITIONAL PARIS DINING —
## AMONG MY FAVORITES ⇐

Yes it's still there as there it long has been — it's just important to separate the famous-name fallen stars from those who have stayed the course with distinction.

My sentimental favorite among the classics is the three-star Ledoyen (Carré des Champs-Elysées), beautifully situated and decorated in what strikes me as more a British than a French woodiness, but there's also a gorgeous terrace where you simply must be for lunch in the appropriate seasons.

Ledoyen began life during the Louis XVI era as a pleasant stop for carriaged travelers in transit seeking simple refreshment, but of course developed into much more. Part of my pleasant first memory of Ledoyen, where I was dining alone, had to do with my choice of the restaurant's famed grilled scallops, to be followed by a rack of young lamb, despite Ledoyen's fame for baked turbot. The apposition of the scallops and the lamb created a problem in wine selection, so I consulted the sommelier, knowing that Ledoyen's was (and is) famed for its cellar. He brought two half-bottles of Saint Emilion, saying "this one for *les coquilles*, the other for *l'agneau*." I wasn't accustomed at the time to have red wine with scallops, but the light one he chose did not overwhelm the mollusks and in fact complimented their searing. The richer one could not have been more perfect with the fragrantly herbed lamb.

I concluded, sommelier's suggestion, with Cognac of uncommon

lightness and fineness, Prince Hubert de Polignac, a label previously unknown to me. Since I was about to leave Paris, I
called Ledoyen the next morning to ask about purchasing a
bottle. "Of course. It will be ready for you by midday." And it was,
tissue-wrapped and neatly bagged. I think you get the sense of
Ledoyen.

There are parallels between Ledoyen and Taillevent (15 rue
Lamennais; odds are the taxi driver won't know this tiny street so
tell him it runs between rue Washington and avenue de Friedland
in the 8th Arrondissement). Taillevent opened in 1946, moved to
its current location in 1950, and was taken over by master restaurateur Jean-Claude Vrinat, son of the founder, in 1962. So there's
tradition here, too. It's not only familial: the wood paneling and
deep colors one might associate with a fine men's club in London
or New York. And M. Vrinat, with his impeccable tailoring and
easy warmth, is the paradigmatic club manager.

Predictably, the clientele at this three-star is largely American,
British, and Asian, but the cooking was staunchly Parisian, if not
adventurous, during the thirty-year reign of chef Claude Deligne.
He's been succeeded at least once, the current incumbent being
Alain Soliveres, who's infused the menu with bright flavor notes
from the south of France. The wine list is extensive and adventurous: Sommelier Marco Pelletier, a Canadian, will guide you
through. While Taillevent is a temple for dark suits and business
deals, I've always dined well here while enjoying the ambience.
Dress well.

## Seeking the Unusual in Dining

You can be a bit more unbuttoned at my favorite upscale bistro, Benot (20 rue Saint-Martin, near the Hôtel-de-Ville in the Marais). It took me a while to discover this delight, which could by its cuisine be in Lyon, and its chef-owner Mchel Petit, who became a friend on my first visit and has remained one. Since 1912, Beroit has remained one of the most accurate of Parisian bistros, from its yellowed-walls and plush red banquettes to its cuisine. Just as you would in Lyon, you'll find such things as blood sausage with apples, various preparations of duck, superb cassoulet, remarkable fresh fish. The best *marquise au chocolat* of my experience is often on the menu. While Benoit's wine list is fairly extensive, I learned early on that the best choices were the unlabeled Beaujolais commissioned by Petit specifically for Benoit.

You simply never know when you venture into a Parisian restaurant, or for that matter a restaurant in any city, now what you'll experience will correspond to what you've been advised or read. For the three I've highlighted for you here in Paris, my intention has been to show that no matter how brilliantly the bright new stars may shine, there are those that have stayed a very long course, and admirably.

# 7

# The Particular Wine World of London

*here are boxes within boxes,* clubs within clubs, and that in brief pretty much describes the British wine trade—"business" would among its members be considered too crass a word—centered of course in London. There are very few players at the highest levels, mostly at the major auction houses and at merchants representing top imports. They don't always get on so well together, somewhat surprising in such a small professional community, similar I suppose to Wall Street. In both places, everyone of note knows each other, with varying degrees of fondness, animosity, or indifference.

But at the top levels of the London world of wine, it's the great sum of the individuals' accumulated expertise and diverse personalities that draws one in, if one is allowed in at all. To be at all a participant, especially as an *auslander,* one must make at least one friend within the circle, as I did with London wine merchant, educator, and author Steven Spurrier. If at some professional wine tasting event in London you're seen as a new face but are perceived as a bit dim by the collective high standard, I'd think you might hear "It's been *lovely* to meet you"—and we'll never see you again.

But Steven set me in with just the right people, precisely the ones I wanted to meet anyway, and we got on well. Those included his great friends Jane MacQuitty, the skilled and witty wine editor of the *London Times*; Oz Clarke, the immensely talented fellow who combines equally successful careers in light opera and wine writing; Jancis Robinson MW, the wine author and her husband, Nick, who were happily operating L'Escargot in Soho just before her writing and broadcast careers took off; the inimitable Hugh Johnson; Michael Broadbent MW, then director of the wine auction department at Christie's; Pat Grubb MW, at the time head of Sotheby's wine department.

There were also more august figures such as the tweedy Edmund Penning-Rowsell, who had covered wine for the *Financial Times* for who knows how many years; the authoritative Harry Waugh, like Michael Broadbent an alumnus of the fine old firm Harvey's of Bristol, and whose tasting recollections in several volumes were edited by Broadbent for Christie's publishing branch; Pamela Van Dyke-Price, prolific author and doyenne of British wine writers. Later I came to know Serena Sutcliffe MW first as a brilliant lecturer on Burgundy at a Sotheby's Burgundy seminar, subsequently as she became head of Sotheby's international wine department. Just a bit farther on I met Serena's husband David Peppercorn MW, a deeply intellectual and wryly humorous man whose expertise on Bordeaux is evident in what I consider one of the best books on the region and its wines, as I consider Ms. Sutcliffe's slimmer summary of Burgundy fact-filled and quite extraordinary.

You'll notice that "MW" is appended to some names and not others. It's the acronym for "Master of Wine," a coveted and hard-won distinction established by the London-based Institute of Masters of Wine, founded in 1960. There are fewer than 250 MWs worldwide, most in the UK, not surprising since until recently one had to have been a full-time member of the UK wine trade for five years before even being allowed to sit for the exam, a harrowing three-day affair of extensive written work and devilishly challenging tastings. Of late, the Institute has taken in members from outside the UK, but very few. Those whose names I've mentioned without MW appended, in most cases, either have not been part of the wine trade, but authors, or in the cases of such elder statesmen as the late Harry Waugh, saw no need to undergo an exam procedure to credential an already distinguished career.

Incidentally, one would have to love Mr. Waugh, even had he not been immensely talented and irrepressibly cheery, for the spirit with which at age sixty-nine he married and found himself the father of twins the next year. "I only hope," Harry said to me somewhat wistfully one afternoon at the Waugh's home in North London, the babies crawling all over him, "that I live long enough for them to remember me." When he eventually passed on at age ninety-seven, acute as ever, the twins were well into adulthood.

His life was testimony for his adage that one must never drink anything less than very good wine, preferably red, and unstintingly.

And if anyone were to think of the MWs as a group of arid academics, that person would be dead wrong. The younger, despite their formidable knowledge, are never ones to turn down a good time. I noted that when I accepted a kind invitation from the Institute to join them at their 1991 Oxford conference and to deliver a short summary on the state of California sparkling wine. The conversation over dinner, as well as the presentations earlier, showed brilliance and a universal articulateness. However, when I emerged from my austere university room to go down for breakfast, I had to pass a table at which one of the younger MWs was holding court, offering everyone who walked by two glasses. One was some nondescript red wine, the other the same wine mixed with straw. "Before breakfast," he said, "here's your final question for the tasting exam. Which is the faulted wine?"

Many younger members of the London wine establishment I met through the aforementioned Steven Spurrier, the more senior ones on introduction by one to another. That part was accelerated by Michael Broadbent's urging, not long after meeting him, that I come over in June 1975 for a quite extraordinary Christie's sale of wines from the Bordeaux First Growths Châteaux Lafite-Rothschild and Mouton-Rothschild, preceded by a private professional tasting of selected vintages. Although I had tasted through several vintages of young claret in barrel, first with 1969s, as described in chapter 1, I had limited exposure to a broad spectrum of older wines because all but the most famous were and are rarely seen outside private collections, except in the London auction market. Reflective tasting of these wines in this environment, I thought, would broaden my horizons importantly.

And so it did. These wines spanned a range of vintages from 1945 to 1971, including both great ('45, '47, '59, '61), not-so-great ('50, '60, '67, '69), and some, such as 1952, better than early reports indicated, in this case because the following 1953 overshadowed it in garnering such praise in its youth. Moreover, all the wines had come directly from the estates' cellars, so each vintage could be clearly evaluated without concern for the storage conditions of the bottles.

Here at Quaglino's Ballroom were all the glorious wines, the older ones decanted, set on white-tableclothed tables to facilitate evaluation of color. And here were several of the more august wine-trade figures, both literary (some of whom I've mentioned) and wholesale/retail. As I slowly proceeded through the wines, youngest to oldest, I relished individual conversations as well as discreetly eavesdropping on others':

"Shame about the '69s, isn't it? So thin and hard, so little fruit. And right after the harvest the Bordeaux boys were touting it as the next '61!"

"But don't forget they were overloaded with two pretty disappointing previous vintages, and they needed a dramatic story."

"Right you are."

(I had to chuckle to myself about that one: q.v. chapter 1.)

"Have you had a look at the '59 Mouton? Damned if it doesn't still have years ahead of it. There's so much fruit and texture to outlast the tannin."

"Yes, I thought it would peak early, but I think it may outlast me!"

"And I might too, the wine aside, old chap!"

Penning-Rowsell: "Such a pretty '48 Lafite. Still there, but not for much longer. Too bad it got caught between the '47 and the '49. No one looked at it."

This '48 Lafite was poured from a Marie-Jeanne, a nearly obsolete format which is the equivalent of three bottles. When I was dining with Steven Spurrier and a group of friends a few years later at the three- (now two-) star Pyramide in Vienne, I was searching the wine list for alternatives to the red Rhônes that dominated it and which we had consumed almost without alternatives over the past days. I handed the list to Steven, and at the bottom of a back page he found the '48 Château Lafite in Marie-Jeanne! The ancient sommelier, undoubtedly miffed that this large table of young non-French had passed over his recommendations of Rhônes and immature Burgundies, said he'd have to check the cellar to see if he still had it. He promptly returned with a bottle, and when Steven asked him how many more were in the cellar the sommelier replied *"J'ai deux Marie-Jeannes en plus, monsieur."* "Excellent," said Steven, "then bring them both." We enjoyed them immensely, but I found these examples a touch less fresh than the one I had sampled at Christie's, direct from Lafite. The late, legendary chef-owner of Pyramide, Fernand Point, must have seen the merits of this wine and put some down not long before his untimely death.

After such a magnificent tasting, naturally I attended the sale, not principally to buy because I thought prices would be stratospheric, but to observe the mechanism and get a sense of the market. A London auction room is pretty straightforward: There is no décor save the occasional display of items for an upcoming arts sale, in which case those pursuing such objects meander through to inspect while the wine sale is ongoing. The auctioneer is at a podium, his associate at a desk nearby monitoring "the book," the carefully recorded bids, lot by lot, of those who are not present but have entered price-limit bids by mail or wire. In important sales, there may be a third person, taking phone bids while the auction is in progress, sometimes on a tie line with an important bidder focused on one particular lot (though that practice is more typical of art sales).

In recent times Christie's and Sotheby's indicate an estimated price range for each lot, and the auctioneer's opening offer may be the lower of those numbers, or it could be the lowest price in the book, if that exceeds what is in the catalog. Bidding proceeds from the floor, against the book and sometimes the telephone, rising in increasing increments as the bid level rises. Eventually, the auctioneer will say something like "I have £190 . . . 190 . . . do I hear £200? £190 on my left . . . going once . . . going twice . . . fair warning at £190 . . ." [Hammer bangs.] "Yours, madam, at £190."

The sale I attended was not typical in that many of the younger wines were being sold in fairly large quantity, in multiple lots of three, five, ten, fifteen, twenty cases of the same vintage. I noted that in some cases the price per lot would gradually decrease as the auctioneer proceeded through the lots on offer, the highest prices being paid by those who believed they wanted this vintage at any reasonable price. Less fervent bidders would sense the floor and bid accordingly. I saw that one hundred cases of '66 Lafite opened at £120 the dozen, but fell by the last lot to £90. I had my eye on the next grouping, forty-two cases of '66 Lafite halves, twenty-four to the box. It opened at £74, went immediately to £78 and then £80, after which it dropped to £74 again. I bid £72 per case for the next-to-last five cases of halves, and got it. So suddenly I owned 120 half bottles of perfectly stored '66 Lafite at essentially $10 each! The only sad part is that they're long gone.

That experience was evidently pleasant for me, but a substantial fraction of those participating in the London market do so in absentia, submitting bids by mail, fax, or phone. I've inferred from questions often asked that some potential buyers think this a dangerous practice, in that the auctioneer could jump to your maximum bid if it were higher than the last one from the floor. That just doesn't happen: The "book" is bidding as carefully for you against the floor as you would be for yourself if present at the sale. If your absentee bid is indeed the highest, you'll have the wine at the smallest increment over the final floor bid, not at your maximum. For instance, I noticed three bottles of a 1911

# Corks & Forks

Corton in a Christie's catalog, and since I was looking for wines from that vintage for my father's seventieth birthday in 1981, I placed a phone bid and did obtain the wine—at substantially less than my maximum.

After the unforgettable encounter with the Lafites and Margaux, I was surprised and delighted when a similar opportunity came my way two years later. While in Bordeaux on a tasting survey, I noticed a newspaper column about an upcoming sale at Christie's of an exceptional range of First Growth Château Latour, the bottles directly from the estate. The column observed that there would be very limited tasting of certain wines the day before the sale, a simple display of bottles on the day before that. I sensed that there might be a bit more, so I took the bull by the horns and wired Michael Broadbent (no e-mails in 1977!) of my interest in attending the sale. By return wire, he said, "You are welcome at Christie's for the Latour sale and for a private professional tasting of the wines on June 14."—two days before the sale. Needless to say, I was in London at the appointed time, and when I saw the wines set forth, I nearly had to pinch myself.

Latour, surely a special favorite of mine and of any Bordeaux fancier, was represented from 1863 to 1974, and most remarkably, in *every single vintage from 1916 to 1974* (not all of those, of course, at the tasting). And taking the measure of the many offered was a small selection of the top echelon of London's wine circle, similar in composition to the Lafite-Margaux tasting group. The conversation, if any, was muted: This event was all about concentration. I began with the 1865, which astonished me with vital red-tawny color, a lively cedar-tinged Cabernet bouquet followed by complex flavors and nearly incredible fruit and body for a wine of such venerability. A marvel! concludes my notes. "Not bad for the year they shot your President Lincoln, don't you think?" whispered an amused Mr. Penning-Rowsell at my elbow. Not bad indeed. Nor were the 1890, a bit thin but showing a gorgeous nose and evident fruit; the fleeting, feminine, but alive 1897; the 1899, much praised in its time, drying a bit but compensating with an ethereal bouquet developed over so many years in perfect cellar storage.

Among the pre-WWII wines, on which I won't dwell because they are virtually out of commerce, I noted a perfectly mature, elegant 1921; an even more youthful, flavory 1922; a 1926, celebrated in its day, still tannic but with fruit in balance. Then there were the famous "twins," 1928 and 1929. Debate used to rage over which was finer, but the debate has diminished as have the ranks of the debaters. Suffice it to say that in 1977, the '28, despite a fully developed bouquet, was still hard, with substantially more tannin than fruit, while the '29, though not as powerful, showed remarkable complexity and finesse. There wasn't much of note from the '30s, almost as if the Bordeaux vineyards were reflecting the contemporary economic and political problems of Europe.

Wartime vintages were also difficult, in part due to shortage of pickers. The end of the war was appropriately marked by the superb 1945, exhibiting plenty of life in 1977 and even in 2000,

when I last saw it, though the intervening years brought gradual decline. A particular standout, the 1949 showed an intricate,
truffly bouquet and glorious flavors, though thinning body indicated a wine at (or a touch beyond) its prime. The next decade was
highlighted by the twin stars 1955 and 1959, the latter promoted
breathlessly in its youth as "the vintage of the century," a phrase
used soon again for 1961 and of course later for 1982. On this
occasion, the '55 was more mature and alluring, while the splen-
didly concentrated '59 indicated that a few more years might be
necessary to reveal its full potential.

Nothing in the '60s excelled the 1961, but then few red Bordeaux of any year could. Richly colored, packed with cedar-tinged
Cabernet flavors, this wine showed beautifully at the tasting and
continues to, with potential well into this century. I noted the
deep and amply constituted 1964 as another gem of the decade,
and I have enjoyed it several times over the years. After all these
older Latours, the 1970 seemed closed and reluctant, though it
has evolved as a lovely if not classic vintage.

If you can imagine, there was more to come. We were invited
for dinner at Brooks's, one of the top Saint James's gentlemen's
clubs, for what was called "A Dinner to Honor 1929 Mouton-
Rothschild." The menu was so spectacular, and such of another
time, that I am compelled to reproduce it for you. Note the
classic simplicity of the food: It was a night for wine to take
center stage.

*The Particular Wine World of London*

## Canapes Stefan II

VEUVE CLICQUOT, 1943, JEROBOAM

## Filets de Sole

RIDGE VINEYARDS CHARDONNAY, 1974

## Selle d'Agneau Roti

CHÂTEAU PALMER, 1924, IMPERIALE

## Soufflé au Fromage

CHÂTEAU MOUTON-ROTHSCHILD, 1929, JEROBOAM

## Melon d'Ogen aux Fraises

CHÂTEAU D'YQUEM, 1924

## Stilton

MARTINEZ, 1897, JUBILEE PORT

## Café

COGNAC, 1865

WHISKY, BLAIR CASTLE, 1835

"And so to bed," as old diaries often conclude their entries. Tastings such as those described, and of course many others of various wine types, have often led me to reflect on what wine tasting at a sophisticated level really entails. Those outside the field often think that a wine "expert" is one who, after a couple sips, can specify the grape variety, the region, and the year. To me, that's reducing evaluation of wine to a party trick. It's most important to understand the wine, to know what it is about, and with exposure to a broad spectrum of wines over time, you might surprise yourself at how close you come to correct conclusions about a given sample.

Some say that the ability to taste wine at a high level is a gift, and to an extent I think that's true. But most important is the same answer given to the child asking a Manhattan pedestrian how to get to Carnegie Hall—practice, practice, practice. That helps you build a taste memory, which comes more easily to some than to others, but is essential to intelligent tasting. If you're given a glass of Sancerre to identify and you say it's a Sauvignon Blanc, probably French, you're doing well, but if you think it's a California Chardonnay, you're not doing so well. A good darts player doesn't always hit the bull's eye, but were he consistently off the board, he'd have cause for concern. If you can choose a grape variety and know why, a likely region of production and why, the approximate age and why, then you're tasting well indeed and will only improve as your breadth of exposure to different wines increases.

In the '80s and '90s, developments in California/Pacific Northwest, Italy, Spain, Australia/New Zealand, and other regions demanded an ever-greater share of my time, so I was in London less frequently than I had been in the earlier stages of my career.

But I did (and do) find myself there often, and I've had ample opportunity to monitor what has and hasn't changed in the London wine world over the past thirty years.

Perhaps the most stunning development was the appointment of Serena Sutcliffe MW as head of Sotheby's international wine department in 1996. "Stunning" not because the brilliant Ms. Sutcliffe wasn't eminently qualified, assuming the post at Sotheby's with nearly thirty years' wine experience as author and at the highest levels of the MW organization, but because the business side of the London wine establishment had forever been the quintessential old boys' club. Under Ms. Sutcliffe's direction, Sotheby's has in recent years overtaken Christie's in wine auction volume, in part because of its success with American sales, including the 1999 New York "Millenium Sale," which at $14.4 million still holds the record for a single wine auction.

There was also a changing of the guard at Christie's, as Michael Broadbent retired (to a schedule as busy as ever, I'd guess) and was succeeded by Anthony Hanson, who came to Christie's from a prominent career as merchant and author, most notably of the groundbreaking 1982 *Burgundy*. It takes courage to begin such a book with the statement "Great Burgundy smells of shit" and then proceed to trample on the iconic toes of Hospices de Beaune, Clos de Vougeot, and Louis Latour, among others, but that Hanson did, contributing in my view to some long-overdue improvements in Burgundian labels that had rested too long on their laurels.

Particularly important over the past twenty years or so has been

# Corks & Forks

the "democratization" of wine in London. Until all too recently, quality wine did not penetrate much below the upper middle class—others could swill their beers. Gentlemen would patronize such venerable establishments as Berry Bros. & Rudd (since 1698) or Justerini & Brooks, conveniently located near their Saint James's clubs, or Corney & Barrow in the City. All that began to change when Seagram opened its chain of Oddbins wine shops, and even more recently with the rapid growth of Majestic, which operates about forty well-stocked outlets throughout London. Now the French mega-chain Nicolas has climbed aboard as well, and their shops seem to be around every third street corner in prime neighborhoods.

So there have been evolutionary changes in the wine world of London. But one senses that the bedrock traditions of the trade will carry on.

## ☞ MICHAEL BROADBENT MW ☜

If you regularly read the London-based magazine *Decanter*, which you surely should since it's the best publication of its type out there, you've undoubtedly seen the cheery figure of Michael on his bicycle, adorning one of his monthly columns, now approaching four hundred, dating from 1978.

Broadbent, trained as an architect, turned to wine in the '50s, became a significant presence at the fine old firm Harvey's of Bristol, and was eventually tapped by Christie's in 1966 to recreate a wine auction program with an international focus. That's how I came to meet him, as related earlier in this chapter.

Always gracious and dapper, now in retirement from Christie's and given more to tweeds and jeans than to well-tailored suits, Michael received me warmly in his office even early in my writing career. But before going off for lunch, often at his club, I quickly learned of his ritual. He'd have a mystery bottle sent to the office as apéritif and to challenge his guest to figure out what it was. One time it was clearly white Burgundy, I thought probably Meursault, which it was, and I knew it had age, which it did, but I couldn't place the vintage. With a chuckle of triumph, Michael said, "You're right about what it is, but it's a 1950!" an off-vintage hardly ever seen then or now. A mischievous Broadbent trick.

But my favorite Michael story has to do with a wine conference organized by the then-principal Italian wine critic Luigi Veronelli. This event was held in some fallen-down medieval castle in Gorizia, just on the border of now Slovenia, and the meeting room had neither windows nor heat in bone-chilling cold. Moreover, most of us were put up in Gradisca, which if you have a magnifier, will show in your atlas as a suburb of Gorizia, if such can be imagined.

We were all dealt lodgings at random, and my wife and I were among the fortunate to be put up in a small hotel in what might be called the center of Gradisca. Michael was not so lucky, spending his time at some little place adjacent to the rail tracks, his sleep impaired more than slightly as the trains rattled by. But typically, he was unflappable and cheery—"stiff upper lip" if you will—despite the conditions.

If you don't already own it, you must have his *Vintage Wine: Fifty Years of Tasting Three Centuries of Wines*, a simply incomparable compilation of tasting notes organized by region, its title being exactly descriptive. Broadbent is famed in the wine community for his collection of tasting notebooks—thus *Vintage Wine*—and part of the process is the participation of Daphne Broadbent. By my good fortune, she was my dinner partner at a festive event at Château Margaux in 1984, and in the course of dinner, she explained the note-taking process. By her account, she often accompanies her husband when he's evaluating wines, notebook in hand, jotting down Michael's comments as he moves from sample to sample.

It's rare that a wine merchant becomes a respected critic, Gerald Asher one of the very few to parallel Broadbent's singular achievements.

### ⌀ SERENA SUTCLIFFE MW
### and DAVID PEPPERCORN MW ⌀

There's no question that each of these major figures on the world wine stage deserves a personal profile, but I've chosen to combine them because they have comparably superb skills at the highest levels of wine assessment, and because they're just so inextricably fun to be around, at a shared house in France, at a London restaurant, at our home in San Francisco or theirs in London.

Serena, for a while a simultaneous translator at UNESCO in Paris, passed the Master of Wine exam in 1976 on her first attempt, thus becoming the second female MW. After a successful career in wine lecturing and writing, including a superb slim and to-the-point guide to the best and less good of Burgundy, she stunned the London wine community and much of the wine world by becoming head of Sotheby's International Wine Department. The surprise had nothing to do with qualification, which was unassailable, but because such a prestigious post had gone to a woman in London's male-dominated wine society. Perhaps an even greater surprise to those gentlemen has been that under Ms. Sutcliffe's direction, importantly in expanding from London to the United States, Sotheby's has become the world leader in wine auction sales.

David became a Master of Wine in 1962 and chaired the organization from 1968 to 1970, additionally serving as chair of the tasting panel for the grueling MW examination for eleven years. Throughout, he kept up his research on Bordeaux, his first book on the subject, *Bordeaux*, appearing in 1982, a third edition in progress, and in my opinion the finest book in English on the subject. The hugely useful *Pocket Guide to the Wines of Bordeaux*, first published in 1986, was expanded in 2002.

Married in 1977, Serena and David, or as they are often referred to irreverently but lovingly in the wine community, the Pepper-cliffes, have quite different personalities. Serena easily combines knowledge with ebullience, a balance clearly contributory to her marketing successes. David seems at first distinctly professorial, rather like the senior tutor you really liked, until you discover the wry, intelligent sense of humor which could only be British. Together, they are an utter, complimentary delight, which it has been our pleasure to appreciate at different times and in various venues.

## ⌒ JANCIS ROBINSON MW ⌒

As I've mentioned, I met Jancis and her husband, Nick, in London through our mutual friend Steven Spurrier. Jancis and I were both pretty much at the early stages of our writing careers, and on first meeting I found her a bit serious but very appealing, a bit like the bookish person who ends up with Cary Grant at the end of the film. She is, after all, a Master of Wine, and that doesn't come without serious study. It was a little later before I discovered how funny she can be, reinforcing my Cary Grant point.

While I was concentrating on my monthly restaurant and wine periodicals, Jancis was directing her attention to books, and what books they are. Her magnum opus is surely the encyclopedic, eleven-hundred-page *Oxford Companion to Wine*, which took her years to compose and edit, and is also aptly titled in that Oxford was Jancis's university. *The Great Wine Book*, superbly written and lavishly illustrated, profiles her choices of top wineries in France (predominantly), Germany, Italy, Spain, California, and Australia. Subsequent was *Tasting Pleasure: Confessions of a Wine Lover*, very much in the structural style of this book, reflecting what she considers most memorable over the course of her lengthy tasting experience and her thoughts on those who made the wines.

Jancis hardly lacks energy, in that she also writes a syndicated newspaper column and does regular television work in the UK. Lots of people are dynamos, but dynamos with great talent are special indeed.

$\backsim 8 \backsim$

# The 1976 Paris Tasting

## *How It Happened and What It Meant*

*O* *n a lazy summer afternoon* in 1975, the phone rang and it was Patricia Gallagher from L'Académie du Vin in Paris. It was a nice surprise, since I had known Patricia and her English business partner, Steven Spurrier, almost since their founding the Academy, which offered top-flight wine courses and the adjacent Les Caves de la Madeleine, one of the best wine shops in Paris, both enterprises particularly unusual because of their joint British-American ownership. It was good news: Patricia was coming to California to choose a few wines for the shop and, incidentally, for a tasting she and Steven were planning to show them off. Could I spend some time with her here and offer advice as to which wineries should be her top priorities during her short stay? Of course I could, and I did, little knowing what would come of those recommendations.

I thought carefully about where to send her, with her limited time and acute palate, knowing that seeing just the wines she wanted would result in rapid decisions. Her and Steven's interests

# The 1976 Paris Tasting

were principally in Chardonnay and Cabernet Sauvignon, in part given their general consideration as California's top varietals, but also because the best could so legitimately be placed for comparative tasting purposes alongside white Burgundies and red Bordeaux, themselves Chardonnays and Cabernet Sauvignon–based, respectively.

For Cabernet Sauvignons, I thought first of Stag's Leap Wine Cellars, a brilliant new Napa Valley property owned by Warren Winiarski (q.v. chapter 2), early on a brilliant political science lecturer at University of Chicago who cast his lot for California, worked at Beaulieu with the legendary André Tschelistcheff, then at the emerging and experimental Robert Mondavi. I thought his own '73 Stag's Leap Wine Cellars Cabernet Sauvignon, as a first effort and in a Bordeaux style, was simply exceptional, and I wanted Patricia to see it. And to further the Bordeaux connection, I thought she should visit Bernard Portet, also in Napa, who had already released a couple Napa Cabernets startlingly suggestive of the Médoc—hardly a major surprise, since Portet had more or less grown up at Château Lafite-Rothschild, where his father had been *régisseur*, or general manager. She already knew the legendary Joe Heitz and his famed "Martha's Vineyard" Cabernets, as she did the "Monte Bello" Cabernets of Paul Draper at Ridge Vineyards farther south in the Santa Cruz mountains, examples of both I believe were already in the Paris shop.

I had a more challenging time with Chardonnay, since the more opulent Californian style was and is difficult to parallel as one might wish it could be with the Burgundian equivalent. The first releases of Chalone, produced from stone-rich hillside vineyards remotely south of San Francisco and interior from Monterey, had produced some stunning, mineraly wines suggestive of the better Meursaults and Pulignys, and I thought Patricia needed to know the current releases. For contrast, I suggested Château Montelena in the northern part of Napa Valley, its first few Chardonnays having impressed me with Burgundian accuracy accented by an extra touch of Californian ripeness. Plus, I knew Montelena's 1882 structure, from Napa's pre-Prohibition golden age of winemaking, would appeal to Patricia's keen esthetic eye.

Upon Patricia's return to Paris, and even after Steven's follow-up visit the next spring, I didn't think much about their intended Paris tasting of top-level California wines and their likely French counterparts. That is, until I had an early-morning call from Steven on May 25, 1976, not long after his return to Paris. "Guess what," he said, "we had the Californian–French tasting yesterday, and the California wines were tops!"

Of course he went on with details, and I had them in front of me in the day's *Herald-Tribune* and only a few days later as a feature in *Time*. It was that important to the international journalistic community that nine of France's best regarded wine figures had blind-tasted a selection of French and Californian Chardonnays and Cabernet Sauvignons and had given first places to the Californians. And it didn't stop there: Of ten Chardonnays assessed, three of the top five places went to California, including first, and among

Cabernets it was first place and two among the top five, the three French reds being First- or Second-Growth Bordeaux.

Looking at the wines and at their tasters is equally interesting, but scanning the wines first shows such a discrepancy in scores that to me this becomes the principal focus. Keep in mind that the tasters were asked to evaluate on a 0–20 scale, so a perfect score for any wine, with nine participants, would have been 180.

### CHARDONNAYS

1973 Château Montelena, Napa Valley (132)

1973 Meursault-Charmes, Domaine Roulot (126.5)

1974 Chalone, Monterey County (121)

1973 Spring Mountain, Napa Valley (104)

1973 Beaune "Clos des Mouches," Drouhin (101)

1972 Freemark Abbey, Napa Valley (100)

1973 Bâtard-Montrachet, Ramonet-Prudhon (94)

1972 Puligny-Montrachet "Les Pucelles," Domaine Leflaive (89)

1972 Veedercrest, Napa Valley (88)

1973 David Bruce, Santa Cruz County (42)

### CABERNET SAUVIGNONS / BORDEAUX

1973 Stag's Leap Wine Cellars, Napa Valley (127.5)

1970 Château Mouton-Rothschild (126)

1970 Château Haut-Brion (125.5)

1970 Château Montrose (122)

1971 Ridge "Monte Bello," Santa Cruz County (103.5)

# Corks & Forks

1971 Château Léoville-Las-Cases (97)
1971 Mayacamas, Napa Valley (89.5)
1972 Clos du Val, Napa Valley (87.5)
1970 Heitz "Martha's Vineyard," Napa Valley (84.5)
1969 Freemark Abbey, Napa Valley (78)

So the logical next step in explaining how all this happened is to put the tasters together with the wines. All were French, all of impeccable achievement and palate. They were Pierre Brejoux, at the time chief inspector of Institut National des Appellations d'Origine (INAO), the organization in charge of France's *appellation controlée* system; Odette Kahn, editor of the influential periodical *La Revue du Vin de France*; Aubert de Villaine, a principal of Domaine de la Romanée-Conti; Raymond Oliver, legendary chef-owner of the three-star Le Grand Vefour; Pierre Tari, proprietor of Château Giscours in Margaux; Christian Vanneque, as chief sommelier at Tour d'Argent presiding over one of the finest cellars in France; Jean-Claude Vrinat, longtime owner of three-star Taillevant; Claude Dubois-Millau of *Le Nouveau Guide Gault-Millau*, Michelin's rival; and Michel Dovaz, a widely published and respected wine journalist.

It's important to put in perspective what these blue-ribbon tasters expected versus what emerged from the experience. They thought, I surely believe, that they were invited for an informal taste-around of Californian and French wines by their good friends Steven and Patricia. And I believe as well that Steven's and Patricia's intention was the same, the subsequent publicity a factor of the stunning results. And they thought that picking out the Californians from the French would be as easy as finding colored eggs on Easter Sunday.

So what was it that made these estimable Paris tasters, undoubtedly enjoying each others' company at an informal event, conclude what they did to shake the wine world? I believe it was natural adherence to what has been called "the French palate," in contrast to "the California palate" much disdained by Europeans, in this instance confounding to the Parisians because the top-scoring California wines had crossed the line into their own tasting territory. Evidently, there is no statistical differentiation among the first three whites, two of them Californian, or among the top four reds, the one in first place being from Napa. But all nine of the tasters gave first-place votes to either of the top-scoring California Chardonnays.

The tasters thought the most favored wines were French because in style they *were*. It was easy for them to dismiss those Californians that for reasons of concentration, alcohol, or tannins they identified as non-French and marked down. But what surprised them and those who looked at the results was that several of the best California wines were sitting on the same pedestal with their French counterparts.

With the immediate and widespread publication of the Paris results, several of the tasters disdained their very own conclusions, with excuses ranging from not understanding the scoring system

# Corks & Forks

to not comprehending the importance given a tasting they thought of no particular consequence. But *le chat* was quite clearly out of *le sac*, like it or not: The best California wines were recognized as playing prominently in the big leagues as they had never been seen before. Even in the twenty-first century, Paris 1976 stands as the event that brought California's best to the world's attention.

## STEVEN SPURRIER

It must have been thirty years ago that Steven and I met, toward the beginning of our respective careers. There was not the prominent actor Hugh Grant then, as there is now, but the correlative is appealing. Through establishing landmark wine ventures in Paris and London, distinguishing himself as one of the finest tasters and writers in the wine world, Spurrier has maintained the boyish good looks that might make you think he was just a few years out of school.

School was Rugby and then London School of Economics. One might not assume that background would lead directly to wine, nor my own at Harvard and Harvard Business School, but that's the professional field Spurrier and I both chose, and we became friends straightaway.

Just as I began a wine newsletter against much advice that it would never succeed, Steven bought in 1970 his *Les Caves de la Madeleine*. That venture was such a success that it led to the next project of Spurrier and his American partner, Patricia Gallagher, L'Académie du Vin, which opened in 1973. The driving idea was that offering wine-tasting courses, in a city where every native believes (mistakenly) to have wine knowledge in the genes, would appeal to visitors and to the occasional Parisian as well. It was very quickly a triumph, hardly hurt at all by its proximity to the American Embassy and the Paris headquarters of IBM.

But aside from his entrepreneurial achievements, what has always interested me most about Spurrier is his superb skill at assessing wine and passing that knowledge along to amateurs, to the extent it's possible, a skill I first saw at the Academy, later at Burgundy seminars in London. At the professional level, however, it's a different matter entirely. One either tastes well and intelligently, or one doesn't. One taster senses immediately the skill or lack of same in another. Conversation is minimal. And tasting acuity does not always have to do with being a winemaker.

That reality came directly to me when Steven and I were both judges at the Mâcon wine competition, one of France's most important. The panel of winemakers he chaired, evaluating red Burgundies, was confused, and mine, looking at Corbières from the southwest of France, were all vintners from the Loire Valley, none of whom had ever tasted a Corbières, much less understanding why an American was chairing the panel. As the event wound down, I visited Steven's table and he mine, and we both nodded in agreement as to which wines were best.

Spurrier's collective experience, and my great professional respect for him, is why I asked him to join my select panel to reevaluate the 1855 Bordeaux classification (s.v. chapter 9). Since then, he has been involved in numerous writing projects and consultancies, including being a selector of the First Class wines for Singapore Airlines. Be assured, First Class does not get any better than on Singapore, and the wine selections of Spurrier and his associates will smooth a long journey.

# 9

# Bordeaux Redux

*1855 Reexamined 140 Years Later*

*fter the unspectacular* 1969s provided my first experience in extensive tasting of young red Bordeaux from
barrel, I made it an annual feature of my monthly
*Private Guide* to survey wines from the previous year's harvest.
That gave me an opportunity to form an overall opinion of the
vintage and to give my readers early advice as to which wines
they might keep most in mind. But I've never believed in offering advice *too* early: My first serious surveys have always been in
the autumn following the year in question, when each château's
component wines have had a few months of marrying in barrel
after their blending (*assemblage*) in the spring. Tasting the new
wines in March or April is nothing more than a hasty snapshot of
a vintage, perhaps out of focus at that because the newly blended
varietal elements can seem disjunctive at first.

As I proceeded from vintage to vintage, I noticed not only the
sometimes profound differences from one to another, but the
more subtle improvements or declines of individual estates over

time. That evolutionary change intrigued me particularly because it raised questions about the contemporary relevance of the sacrosanct 1855 classification of Médocs and even of the more recent 1953/1959 Graves ranking. If I had seen such evident quality changes among estates over twenty-odd years, how must current performance differ from that immortalized so many years earlier?

I decided to have another look, one that would be based on the tasting opinions of critics beyond reproach on the merits of two highly regarded latter-day vintages. That idea in itself presented at least four initial challenges: to select the vintages for assessment; to access the wines directly from the châteaux so that there could be no question of perfect storage; to choose an international panel of judges with impeccable credentials; and to find a sponsor who would share my view that any financial benefit created should flow to an important charity.

Had I not dealt with the last challenge first, the other three would have been irrelevant. I proposed the concept to Gordon Getty, whom I knew as a serious wine buff and devoted patron of the arts. After one pleasant meeting, Mr. Getty agreed to underwrite the event on behalf of the San Francisco Symphony, which would receive the proceeds of a concluding dinner and the substantial contributions of a very few amateurs invited to taste these wines alongside the professionals, their scores of course not to be tabulated. With Mr. Getty's support, I could proceed to implementation.

# Bordeaux Redux

For the wines, I selected two contemporary but very different vintages, 1986 and 1990. The 1986 crop was more classic in style, the wines all about structure in their earliest years despite a bountiful harvest, the best evolving nicely as they approached the ten-year mark, tannins receding to reveal the fruit they had preserved. In contrast, the 1990's, in retrospect the best clarets of their decade, were immediately charming and much ballyhooed in the press within a year after they were made. I thought these two excellent but dissimilar vintages would indicate the current state of the classified properties.

And those estates were not immediately forthcoming to cooperate, as I had suspected they might not be. The 1855 classification, a commercial promotion devised by ministers of Emperor Napoleon III for a Paris trade fair of its year, was meant to advance the cause of the Médoc reds, hardly seen then with the luster they subsequently acquired. So even though Napoleon's marketing gambit worked, the rankings of the wines were never based on careful tastings, but rather on comparative recent prices submitted by Bordeaux brokers. Yet the five-tier classification, based on nineteenth-century price relationships rather than on contemporary differentiation of intrinsic quality, continued to direct market perceptions and therefore prices for decades upon decades. There was little motivation for château owners to work with me on my project, since some at the 1855 top might be shown not to belong there anymore, while lower classed growths showing better could have their improvement dismissed for its being based on an American tasting, not one conducted by the French Institut Nationale des Appellations d'Origine (INAO), which would have the only official authority to change what had been thrown together by a bunch of brokers back in the 1850s.

The three Bordeaux brokers I knew best all declined cooperation, on the basis of political sensitivity within the community on which their businesses depended. However, I found a strong ally in Sacha Lichine, son of the famed Alexis, who had grown up between New York and Bordeaux, eventually settling there to overlook Château Prieuré-Lichine and to establish his own *négociant* business to find and market regional French wines throughout Europe. Sacha was enthusiastic about my idea and agreed to source the wines needed, but wisely advised that I would need a strong supporter within the classed-growth group for the project to go forward.

I immediately thought of Bruno Prats, one of the most forward-thinking Médoc owners I knew, whose Château Cos d'Estournel had progressed under his direction so that by the 1990s it was widely considered among the so-called "super seconds," such as Château Léoville-Las-Cases and Château Pichon-Lalande, estates placed in the second of the five 1855 tiers but on contemporary achievement thought more appropriately placed in the first. Bruno Prats was also at the time president of Union des Grands Crus de Bordeaux, the organization of classed growths that promotes the singularity, and by extension superiority, of the grouping.

To my delight, M. Prats gave his endorsement, on two conditions.

The first required my word that the project would never be referred to intentionally as a "reclassification." I readily gave assurance, having no intention of using sensitive terminology that would negatively affect his and my relationships in Bordeaux, while also being in technical violation of French law. His second concern was the composition of the tasting panel, which I surely agreed should bring collective credentials beyond reproach.

I thought of those whose critical work I had most admired over the past twenty years, wanting a group of no more than ten, since I was seeking incisive commentary rather than focus-group diffusion. Except for two or three with schedule conflicts, a week in San Francisco being necessary, everyone I invited accepted rapidly. As I received the responses, I began to think about the conjunction of personalities. I knew each person individually, of course, and they knew each other either directly or by reputation. But I wondered how as a group, each at the top of his or her profession, they would interact.

The panel I chaired included Michel Bettane, editor of *La Revue du Vin de France*; Alexis Bespaloff, widely read columnist and author of the revised *Frank Schoonmaker Wine Encyclopedia*; Anthony Dias Blue, wine and spirits editor of *Bon Appétit*; James Halliday, the most noted Australian wine author, and a vintner there as well; Mary Ewing Mulligan MW, then director of the International Wine Center in New York; David Peppercorn MW, noted English author specializing in Bordeaux; Frank Prial, wine editor of the *New York Times*; Steven

# Corks & Forks

Spurrier, London-based writer and conceiver of the famed French-Californian wine comparison (q.v. chapter 8); and Serena Sutcliffe MW, head of Sotheby's international wine department.

While the panelists were making their travel plans, I was worrying over the wines. Sacha Lichine, with whom I was in contact at least once a day at the critical phase of assembling the wines from the various châteaux, had done a superb job, but I wouldn't rest easily until I could see the cases emerge from their refrigerated ocean container safe and sound on a San Francisco pier. Finally that day arrived, a month before the event, and I happily fulfilled my promise to Gordon Getty that we'd watch the wines unloaded from container to warehouse and pull the cork on a random bottle to celebrate what we had done together.

Everyone arrived from their respective cities right on time, a marvel, and we enjoyed an informal Sunday dinner in anticipation of beginning serious work the next morning, January 16, 1995. I had decided to begin with a flight of fourteen *crus bourgeois*, or well regarded Médocs not included in the 1855 list, my choices being wines I had found excellent performers in recent good vintages. I opted for 1990 as the year I thought would show better in this category than 1986, and I also wanted to see how the panelists would use the numerical rating scale I had set forth, before the greater wines were on the table.

I knew the question of numerical rating would cause a stir, since these experts were used to two scales: 0–20, from the 1976 Paris Tasting, or 0–100, as popularized and used by Robert Parker and *Wine Spectator*. The principal problem with the 100-point scale, whoever employs it, is that virtually any wine starts at 50 for simply being uncorked, so the scale is really 50–100 rather than 0–100. Numerical scores are immediately clear to those thinking back to how arithmetic papers were graded in school. But what too many do not understand, or choose to ignore, is that a score for something as subjective as wine is only a quick summary of what the critic or panel of critics thinks, the most important aspect being the tasting note that follows the number. That descriptor will imply, especially as written by the most respected critics, whether you are likely to enjoy the wine or not. You might prefer a wine rated 75 to one at 92, each well made, but you won't know if you buy solely by the numbers. You could prefer Monet to Delacroix, but with a trained eye you will recognize the mastery of each.

That approach was what I wanted to be certain all panelists understood as we sat down to have a look at these fourteen *crus bourgeois* in unmarked glasses. My instruction was that a 20-point or a 100-point scale could be used, the 20-point scores to be multiplied by five to conform to the 100-point scores, and that the scale in each case was to begin with zero. Here were fourteen very creditable wines, tasted by some of the top professionals in the wine world, and the scores overall ranged from 28 to 90, with a clustering in the low 70s. Even more striking to me was that the wine given 28 on one score sheet received 85 on another. But the judge who gave the low score had a solid reason why, as did the colleague who awarded the higher one. Two individuals with acute palates therefore differed principally on the basis of personal taste.

Our next two flights comprised the classed Graves, and once those results came in I saw a pattern comparable to what had come forth with the *crus bourgeois*. For one 1990 the scores were from 44 to 84, while for another, almost all scores were in the 90s, except for one at 75. I thought there was need for a statistician, given the disparity among the raw scores, so I retained one.

The rest of the tasting was serious work, as we progressed through the Médocs, the only mirthful break being a mid-week dinner graciously hosted by Gordon and Ann Getty at their home. Of course there were memorable comments in the course of the tastings, given the personalities of the participants. I think my favorite had to do with a Margaux about which one panelist said, "It isn't lovely, but it's so very, very Margaux." From across the table came, "So how do they make it taste like vomit?"

At the end of the week, just as I was adjusting my black tie in advance of the concluding dinner, the statistician arrived with his analysis, and I was aghast. From First, Château Pichon-Longueville-Baron, Pauillac, a Second in 1855, to the last, Château Croizet-Bages, a Fifth back then, there was a simple and gradual decline in scores, nothing on a statistical basis that would create any groupings at all. I was about to address three hundred people to announce what our master tasters had seen as a rational recalibration of the original rankings. I was not expecting to announce that those rankings had substantially less relevance than they might once have had, or that they now had limited relevance at best. But that is what as a panel we concluded, and that is what I said.

Back upstairs, just untying that tie, the phone began to ring. Press from France and the United States clamored for details, centered on the most sensational question—had the 1855 classification been changed, or dismissed altogether? Over and over, I explained that reclassification could only be accomplished by the French government and its INAO. Yes, Château Lynch-Bages, a Fifth in 1855, had scored ahead of the First Growths Mouton-Rothschild and Lafite-Rothschild, but so did eight other wines in the case of Mouton and twelve that outpointed Lafite. Yes, except for Château Margaux and Château Palmer, Margaux as a group showed dismally. And yes indeed, the 1995 San Francisco reevaluation had cast serious doubt on the established classifications of Médocs and Graves.

Having invested considerable energy in this project, for important result, I wanted to check on its continuing validity. I decided first to survey red Bordeaux of 2001, a serviceable if not great vintage, to determine parallels or dissimilarities among those wines and the 1986s and 1990s we had evaluated. I found striking congruence between certain wines we had been surprised to favor strongly in those vintages and their 2001 counterparts. As examples, the Margaux estates Giscours and Lascombes performed above most of their peers in the 1995 tasting, as did Châteaux Gruaud-Larose in Saint-Julien and Pape-Clément in Graves. All had high marks from me for their 2001s.

My second approach was to think back to 1855 and how those

Corks Forks

brokers had constructed their five-tier scheme on price, not perceived excellence in the glass. So I looked at *Decanter's* report on how First through Fifth Growths of 1986 and 1990 had sold at London auction as recently as January 2004. The prices, in pounds per case and averaged among wines in each category, are startling.

|  | *1986* | *1990* |
|---|---|---|
| FIRSTS | 1828 | 2294 |
| SECONDS | 529 | 731 |
| THIRDS | 407 | 522 |
| FOURTHS | 370 | 361 |
| FIFTHS | 395 | 483 |

That compilation indicates that the official classification is partially a self-fulfilling prophecy, in that the First Growths command more money because they are that by fiat and acclaim, the Seconds a substantial tier below but still more valued than those below. That's just the way the 1855 brokers saw it, but our 1995 reexamination, based on skilled tasting, did not confirm that assessment. It also suggests that trying to determine a hierarchy within the maelstrom of Third to Fifth Growths, by tasting or price, is an exercise in futility. You'll note that in scanning the results of the 1995 tasting, appended.

So as a consumer, what conclusions do you draw in making your own Bordeaux buying decisions? I think they are clear. If you are committed to First Growths just because of their designation, then surely pursue them, if you're not concerned about their significant price premiums. Otherwise explore among the Seconds, being assured that many will excel the Firsts. You can find unexpected treasures within the uncertain territory of the Thirds through Fifths, but here you need the expertise of someone who tastes the wines regularly, Robert Parker in my view your best choice as adviser. Do remember to read past anyone's score to the tasting note, to ascertain if the critic's personal tastes correspond to yours in how you might enjoy the wine.

## The First International Wine Classic

Results of Tasting the 1986 and 1990 Classed Growth Bordeaux

*These wines, representing all the classified growths of the Médoc according to the 1855 grouping, and the Graves as classified in 1953/1959, were tasted over a four-day period in San Francisco in the 1986 and 1990 vintages. The scores of the ten-person international panel of note were averaged, with the highest and lowest scores for each wine dismissed. The resulting mean score for each wine was once again averaged with the score for the other vintage to produce an overall result.*

90.5  Château Pichon-Longueville-Baron, Pauillac (2nd)
90.2  Château Léoville-Las-Cases, St-Julien (2nd)
89.4  Château Haut-Brion (1st)
87    Château Pichon-Lalande, Pauillac (2nd)
86.7  Château Margaux, Margaux (1st)
86.3  Château Cos-d'Estournel, St-Estèphe (2nd)
85.8  Château Latour, Pauillac (1st)

# Corks & Forks

85.1   Château Lynch-Bages, Pauillac (5th)

84.4   Château Léoville-Barton, St-Julien (2nd)

83.6   Château Mouton-Rothschild (1st as of 1973)

83.5   Château Léoville-Poyferré, St-Julien (2nd)

82.4   Château Ducru-Beaucaillou, St-Julien (2nd)

82.2   Château Montrose, St-Estèphe (2nd)

81.6   Château Lafite-Rothschild, Pauillac (1st)

80.5   Château Palmer, Cantenac-Margaux (3rd)

80     Château Saint-Pierre, St-Julien (4th)

78.9   Château Rausan-Ségla, Margaux (2nd)

78.6   Château Gruaud-Larose, St-Julien (2nd)

77.5   Château Langoa-Barton, St-Julien (3rd)°

76.9   Château Cos Labory, St-Estèphe (5th)

76.7   Chateau Calon-Ségur, St-Estèphe (3rd)

76.5   Château Grand-Puy-Lacoste, Pauillac (5th)

76.4   Château Clerc-Milon, Pauillac (5th)

76.2   Château Branaire, St-Julien (4th)

75.3   Château Marquis-de-Terme, Margaux (4th)

75.1   Château Lagrange, St-Julien (3rd)

75     Château Beychevelle, St-Julien (4th)

74.8   Château Giscours, Labarde-Margaux (3rd)°°

74.8   Château Lafon-Rochet, St-Estèphe (4th)

74.8   Château Haut-Bages-Libéral, Pauillac (5th)

74.7   Château Duhart-Milon-Rothschild, Pauillac (4th)

74.3   Château Lascombes, Margaux (2nd)

74.2   Château La Lagune, Ludon (3rd)

74.2   Château Talbot, St-Julien (4th)

74.1  Château Brane-Cantenac, Cantenac-Margaux (2nd)

73.9  Château Mouton-Baronne-Phillippe (1986), Pauillac (5th)

73.9  Château d'Armailhac (1990), Pauillac (5th)***

71.8  Château Grand-Puy-Ducasse, Pauillac (5th)

71.8  Château Belgrave, Pauillac (5th)

71.7  Château Desmirail, Margaux (3rd)

70.8  Château Batailley, Pauillac (5th)

68.5  Château Durfort, Margaux (2nd)

68.5  Château Lynch-Moussas, Pauillac (5th)

68.2  Château Marquis-d'Alesme, Margaux (3rd)

68.1  Château Malescot-Saint-Exupéry, Margaux (3rd)

67.4  Château Prieuré-Lichine, Cantenac-Margaux (4th)

67    Château Haut-Batailley, Pauillac (5th)

66.7  Château Pouget, Cantenac-Margaux (4th)

66.2  Château Cantenac-Brown, Cantenac-Margaux (3rd)

66    Château Pédesclaux, Pauillac (5th)

65.4  Château Boyd-Cantenac, Margaux (3rd)

65.3  Château Cantemerle, Macau (5th)

64.8  Château Pontet-Canet, Pauillac (5th)

64.5  Château Dauzac, Labarde-Margaux (5th)*

64    Château Rauzan-Gassies, Margaux (2nd)

62.6  Château Ferrière, Margaux (3rd)*

62.4  Château du Tertre, Arsac-Margaux (5th)

61.3  Château d'Issan, Cantenac-Margaux (3rd)

57.3  Château La Tour-Carnet, St-Laurent (4th)

56.3  Château Camensac, St-Laurent (5th)

51.7  Château Croizet-Bages, Pauillac (5th)

*1953/1959 Official Classification of Graves as tasted in the 1986
and 1990 vintages*

89.4  Château Haut-Brion

85    Château La Mission-Haut-Brion

77.6  Château Pape-Clément

74.4  Château La Tour-Martillac

74.1  Domaine de Chevalier

73.6  Château Olivier

72.9  Château Carbonnieux

70.9  Château La Tour-Haut-Brion

70.8  Château Fieuzal

70.3  Château Smith-Haut-Lafitte

68.7  Château Malartic-Lagravière

68.2  Château Bouscaut

° Tasted in the 1990 vintage only.

°° Tasted in the 1986 vintage only.

°°° Changed name between the two vintages.

*Château Kirwan (Cantenac-Margaux) and Château Haut-Bailly (Graves)
both asked specifically not to be included in this comparative tasting.*

# 10

# The Fascination of Alsace

*irst thing you have* to understand about Alsace is that it is real, not the theme park it seems. The cobbled streets and timbered houses have been there for centuries, and real people lead bustling lives in the old environs. You would be hard pressed to find a prettier place to visit than this northeastern part of France, at once purely French but closely allied in heritage to its German neighbor.

That's easy to understand when you look at the history. The territory, referred to often as Alsace-Lorraine, has regularly passed between France and Germany, key periods being the end of the Thirty Years' War when Louis XIV acquired it as part of the Treaty of Westphalia in 1648; a reversion to Germany after the Franco-Prussian war in 1871; and back to France again via the Treaty of Versailles in 1919.

Yet Alsace has also cherished its own identity, which is a unique blend of French and German, no better expressed than in its language, a mysterious harmony of those tongues which a visitor might as well pass by in favor of French, German, or English,

# Corks & Forks

which are readily understood in the main towns. Those, for certain, are Ribeauvillé and Riquewihr.

F. E. Trimbach set up shop in 1626 in Ribeauvillé, and by all reports rapidly became one of the most respected wine houses in the region, through a combination of superbly situated vineyards and excellent winemaking. It was such pleasure to be received by Hubert Trimbach on my first visit. Blond, blue-eyed, and brimming with energy and good humor, Hubert couldn't wait to show his beautiful vineyards, explaining the specialness of each.

Then he took us to the cellars, where we met his less effusive but equally charming brother Bernard, winemaker and cellarmaster. While Hubert seems most focused on the vineyards and the finished product, Bernard (and now his sons) want you to understand the process by which the great Trimbach grapes become what you enjoy in bottle.

First, Bernard ran through the nomenclature process, which is varietal, subsequently geographical, and then vineyard specific. That's quite related to Germany, but not to most of the rest of France, where wines are identified by region. For example, if you choose a Sancerre from the Loire Valley, it is a Sauvignon Blanc by definition, though the grape variety is rarely stated on the label.

But as Bernard so carefully explained, the grape variety is the definitional point on Alsace labels, sometimes with vineyard specification and always with denotation of "reserve" Rieslings and Gewurztraminers, as in Germany. After tasting through the full spectrum from Pinot Blanc and Pinot Gris to the richest

Rieslings and Gewurztraminers, I found that the most notable
wines, the "reserves," were those with the greatest concentration
of fruit character, as in Trimbach's rightly celebrated Riesling Clos
Ste. Hune. They all shone forth without emphasis on residual
sweetness, which is prized in the same varietals in Germany and
simply reflective of a different stylistic approach across the
German–French border, clearly expressed at Trimbach.

Then came a most welcome but uncommon invitation, for dinner *en famille*, an evening at Bernard's home. That sort of invitation is rarely extended in France, most entertainment of visitors
taking place in restaurants. So what I was privileged to experience
was the Trimbachs at home, the kids eventually becoming comfortable with the mysterious American. And they delighted as I
did in the best *tarte aux oignons* imaginable, so much finer when
well executed than the more familiar Quiche Lorraine, and by a
*coq au Riesling* distinguished by both the quality of the bird and
by the platter of homemade noodles, light but flavorful, suggest-
ing that Germany was not far away, geographically or gastronomi-
cally, but that French charm prevailed.

Although Ribeauvillé and Riquewihr are pretty close on the
narrow road running north–south, Riquewihr is the more picturesque, while Kayserberg, just a touch south of them, is arguably
the prettiest of the region's eye-catching towns. But Riquewihr
is home to Hugel, vintners since the fifteenth century and one
of the very best. Johnny Hugel, as he is called, the current major
force at the winery, will almost certainly start by showing you the

# Corks & Forks

huge cask in service since 1715, underscoring Alsatian disdain for new oak, improper for their fresh whites anyway. Hugel makes an admirable range of such wines, but also offers highly extracted and extraordinary sweet wines, examples being the *Vendange Tardive* (Late Harvest) Rieslings and Gewurztraminers.

From the outset, I found dining in Alsace a challenge, none-theless a pleasant one. If you're invited, it will almost certainly be to L'Auberge de l'Ill, the region's Michelin three-star. To start, it's a restaurant from the '50s, which features what Calvin Trillin would call "stuff with heavy." Worse though, for me anyway, is the emphasis on foie gras, the local specialty that your host will surely select, and to which I have the same aversion I do to the poached egg, the only two food items I simply will not eat. On your own in local cafés, surely avoid *choucroute garnie,* the local specialty of sausages in a mish-mash of cabbage, a horrible conception never well presented, and that goes for Brasserie Lipp in Paris as well. Stick with *coq au Riesling,* though it is unlikely to be as fine as that *chez* Trimbach, and wash it down with the youngest possible Edelzwicker, preferably from carafe, as Alsatians do.

# 11

# "You Review Restaurants! What Fun!"

*ell, yes it can be,* but in my thirty years of experience on the job, the disappointments far exceed the excitements, and readers are quite properly not much interested in the losers, unless PR has taken some places to a moment of notoriety. The critic's task, and a difficult one, is to separate the winners from the forgettable, usually early in a restaurant's life.

Also there's the factor of excess, by which I don't mean overeating, but the sheer expenditure of energy in visiting three to five restaurants in an evening, which I seldom but sometimes have done. If the first two or three are useless, it's necessary to press on, or the evening is wasted.

Naturally, as a critic, anonymity is essential. One makes reservations using a false name and pays in cash. The importance of that approach was made clear on a visit to Julius Castle, an old-line San Francisco view restaurant where I was entertaining a visitor from Boston but also checking on current performance. She was craving the whitest of veal and a top-level Cabernet.

# Corks & Forks

The first two bottles I selected were out of stock, and the third was utterly spoiled. Meanwhile, the "veal" was a bloody-red beef tenderloin, and when I complained, the owner asked us to leave, no check. I wrote about the experience in my newsletter just as I have done here. Sometime later I encountered Julius Castle's owner at a popular bistro, where he said, menacingly, "Aren't you that critic who wrote such bad things about my restaurant?" "Wrong guy," I said, beating a hasty retreat.

I did pretty much the same thing in leaving a well-regarded Chinatown restaurant I was reviewing when a stir-fried cockroach appeared on a plate of noodles. When I pointed this out to the waiter, he said, with a smile, "no extra charge."

On a grander note, you can be just as disappointed at famous places. For my fiftieth birthday, I selected Lucas-Carton in Paris because I had so appreciated its classic three-star cooking, and the work of its subsequent owner, Alain Senderens, from L'Archestrate, where he brilliantly infused Asian touches into classic French cuisine. But this meal was an utter disaster from the first course to the second, at which point I asked for the check, presented with no question as to how the food had been unsatisfactory. Similarly, our meal at the then two-star Guy Savoy was a comparable wreck, the man himself apparently more devoted to his chain of Paris bistros.

Yet a smile comes from a dinner at Dawat, an admirable Indian restaurant on 58th Street near 3rd Avenue in Manhattan, its menu much influenced by Madhur Jaffrey, whose writings resonate not only in my mind but very often on my stove. It was my second or third time there, and I noticed Bryan Miller, then restaurant critic of the *New York Times*. I went over to say hello, and he asked, "What do you order here?" I told him my favorites and went on with the evening. A few days later his review appeared, with three stars. Better still, the next time at Dawat I was treated like a *maharaja*, being mistaken for Bryan, because of the similarity between my order and his on the same night.

Two things stand out to me in being a responsible restaurant critic. Most obviously, it's being dispassionate, even if you know the owner or have been given good treatment previously or have heard positive (or negative) comments from others. Second is the homework, which involves books and articles on international cuisines, amplified most importantly by direct tasting experience. Being accurate in evaluating a new Thai restaurant, for example, means knowing the cultural history of the cuisine and evaluating any dish versus comparable versions at other restaurants, some preferably in Thailand. The same rubric pertains to the cuisines of any nation, including our own, and their regional variations.

So restaurant criticism, despite how much fun it seems in concept to many, is really concentrated work if done properly, the pleasures on balance much outweighing in memory those frequent disappointments, quickly forgotten. I'm often asked my favorite restaurant in a particular city, a question impossible to answer as simply as it is posed. My best advice is to concentrate on those restaurants, major or minor, where the chef is owner or major partner and spends most of his or her time on premise. Absentee ownership in a business based so much on individual talent very seldom works. Read Las Vegas.

# 12

# My Worst Nightmares
# on the Wine and Food Front

*or all the superb experiences* which have been such a pleasure to enjoy over time, there have been a few I'd have
as soon not had. Here's a selection.

### ☞ Dateline: Nowhere, Japan ☜

Since my initial management-consulting activities took me frequently to Asia, and most often to Japan, I decided to learn something of the language. I spent two years of Saturday mornings at
University of California extension classes, and as time and my
travel went on, I saw progress. Finally I thought it was time to
venture into the Japanese countryside, where English was absolutely not spoken. With a weekend free, I decided on Matsushima,
a historic archipelago two hundred miles north of Tokyo, its tiny
islands connected by picturesque red lacquer bridges, the cave-
dotted islands themselves important meditation sites for monks
who settled there around the ninth century. I thought it would be
a fine place to put my new Nikon through its paces.

# Corks & Forks

My first stop was at the Japan Tourist Bureau office in my hotel, where I told the agent I'd like her to book me a weekend at an inn in Matsushima. After a short look of incredulity, she began to laugh, covering her mouth with the back of her hand, the *politesse* traditional among Japanese women. It was late winter in Tokyo, and I knew it would be even colder farther north, but no matter. The transaction was completed, she thinking my request was about as sensible as asking in Boston in February for a weekend jaunt to Caribou, Maine. I was routed by train to Sendai, the nearest large town to Matsushima, from which I would taxi to my inn chosen by the tourist bureau.

The train was an experience in itself. From subways to mainliners, Japanese trains are usually overcrowded, and this one was no exception. Through a problem with my ticket, or quite possibly my lack of understanding, I started with standing room, and at the next stop was banished to standing room between cars on the frigid ride to Sendai. Once there, pretty much frozen through, I found a taxi driver willing to brave the snowy road to Matsushima, and it surely didn't bother me that he had another passenger up front. But it quickly became clear that they knew each other and didn't get along. The driver stopped abruptly, opened the passenger door and tossed the lady into a snowbank. With no words exchanged, we went on to Matsushima.

Now colder than ever, I was looking forward to something like the inn (*ryokan*) experience so memorable from Kyoto, where a lovely hostess had ushered me through elegant and soundless corridors to my room, then promptly to a vast bath, where I soaked in a superheated tub until being scrubbed and then escorted back to my room, to find the first courses of an elaborate *kaiseki* meal awaiting. Not so in Matsushima. When the taxi dropped me at a rickety building, I was greeted by the gruff proprietor, slow from sleep, who showed me to what he said was a *gaijin* (foreigner) room, distinguished by a space heater, its red coils garish in the darkness. It didn't do much to warm either me or the nearly frozen futon on which I tried to sleep. At first light I looked for the bath, which at that time in rural Japan meant communal—men, women, and children splashing around naked and ebullient—until they noted the entrance of a blond, blue-eyed *gaijin*. They went silent and stared. And *stared*.

Warm at last, I thought it time to explore the village, and I snapped away at the bridges, caves, rice fields, and fishing boats. After a while I thought the Nikon's shutter button was becoming sluggish from the cold, but when I realized it was in fact my shutter finger, I decided to take a break for lunch. Not knowing anything about the options in the village, I simply followed my nose, which led me to a homey little place obviously popular with locals. A teenaged server seated me and brought life-giving hot tea.

Then I realized I had a problem. The menu was chalked on the earthen wall, and despite my studies in conversational Japanese, I hadn't been taught how to read a thing. I had picked up the characters for "entrance" and "exit," "gents" and "ladies," but that was it. So I thought my strategy would be to wait, hands cupped around the warmth of the tea cup, until I saw something familiar pass from the kitchen, and order that. Pretty soon I saw two bowls of *oyako donburi*, an omelette with chicken and green onions over a bowl of rice. They were delivered to an elegant old-style couple across the room, both dressed traditionally and seated, straight-backed, on mats.

So catching the eye of the server, I said in my best Berkeley Japanese, *"are-to onaji mono, kudasai,"* or "Please bring me the same thing." But, horribly, she misinterpreted what I've been told was correct, and thought I wanted *that thing*, not *the same thing*. So she went to their table, and after a brief conversation and glances my way, picked up their bowls and brought them to me.

Now, I thought, what should I do? Is returning the bowls an insult, an indication that they weren't good enough? Or should I order them two new *donburi*? That's what I did, picked at theirs, paid the bill and left as soon as possible, in doing so passing by their table. They rose from their mats, smiled, and bowed extensively.

I did the same, picked up my things at the so-called *ryokan*, and caught the next train back to Tokyo, some excellent photos, two *donburi*, and maybe some international diplomacy to the good.

## Attack of the Chevaliers de Tastevin

The Chevaliers de Tastevin are purportedly a harmless group of well-heeled consumers who meet periodically for happy dinners in their various chapters around the world, to hoist a glass or two in honor of Burgundy. I didn't see any harm in joining the San Francisco satellite when invited, and a few lunches and dinners were indeed pleasant. But if you're a Chevalier, you eventually want to attend the *chapitre*, in essence the annual meeting, held at the mother church, Clos de Vougeot in Burgundy.

The imposing enclosed *clos* (estate) was established by Cistercian monks in the thirteenth and fourteenth centuries, seized from them during the Revolution, and eventually passed to an assemblage of private hands, as were its vineyards. Old politics aside, it's a swell place for a fine party, which the *chapitre* represents, with its procession of Burgundian classic dishes and wines, and its international attendance. There's also periodic entertainment by a group of elderly gentlemen singing traditional local songs, and incessant speeches by regional politicians that become ever more rambling as the evening progresses.

That's all in good fun, or at least so I thought until the final speech. This tipsy gentleman noted numerous English and Japanese attendees, the former he described as having lots of taste but no money, the latter possessing plenty of money but no taste. He went on to give his assessment of rising wine prices as resulting from actions of the Rothschild family because they were Jews.

At this point, revulsed, I stood up and said, *"C'est suffi"* ("That's enough"), and left the dining room while tossing my ceremonial *tastevin*, or tasting cup, on the stage. As I passed through an anteroom on the way to my car, followed by my party, I was set upon by robed Chevaliers, some of whom had just been singing, and their beating was hurting me badly. Seeing that, the other male member of my group, a former champion boxer as a Marine, knocked out my principal attacker with one punch. We headed to our car and back to our hotel.

But I had suffered a broken tailbone and had to cut short my French trip to return to San Francisco, standing up on the plane, for treatment. Did I ever receive an apology from the Chevaliers? No, just a summary dismissal from the organization, which I framed and treasure.

## ⌖ A Missed Connection at Château d'Yquem ⌖

Particularly early on in your wine career, you feel honored to receive a letter from the owner of such a famous property, the most famed of Sauternes, that you would indeed be welcome for your intended visit to the estate.

On the day, I was driving up from Spain, so logically I was stopping first in Sauternes before going on to my hotel farther north near Bordeaux. At d'Yquem, I was received by the courtly general manager, Pierre Meslier, who had absolutely no idea about me or my planned visit, explaining that Count Alexandre de Lur-Saluces, the proprietor with whom I had corresponded, was absent.

But M. Meslier graciously showed me through the property, carefully explaining the winemaking process, in the course of which he led me through a spacious but empty tasting room, with every great vintage of d'Yquem from 1921 arranged in line on an elegant table. Sensing my glance, M. Meslier said, "The Count is expecting a prominent American wine expert," while offering me a glass of the current release. Who could that be? I thought. Alexis Bespaloff was the only American critic I could think of, at that time, who might merit such a tasting, but I knew Alex was not in France.

It all became clear when I arrived at my hotel. There was a handwritten note from the Count de Lur-Saluces delivered on the day before. "I'm terribly sorry, but important business in Bordeaux takes me away from d'Yquem tomorrow morning. Could you possibly come after lunch? I've arranged a tasting I think you'll enjoy!"

Of course I was back in my car right away, on the way to one of the most memorable tastings of my life. There was first of all the Count himself, gently reflective of centuries of French culture, and of course the wines. We both were compelled by the standouts, such as the '21, '28 and '29, which Alexandre must have known as well as he did his comfortably tailored tweed jacket. But he guided me toward the '48, not dramatic but very lovely, and toward another look at the '67, about which I had first written a bit negatively but saw then (and subsequently) as a wine that simply needed time to evolve as a classic.

A premature turn in the morning had become something quite different by the end of the day.

# Corks & Forks

## ❧ Sancerre: Not for the Faint of Heart ❧

It has long been my practice in smaller wine regions to choose wineries for visits based on their appearance on the wine lists of outstanding local restaurants. That approach has worked for me over and over.

After a lunch in the Loire enhanced by a particularly pleasant Sancerre, I decided to call the vintner to arrange an appointment, which he suggested for late that afternoon, suiting me perfectly. He was the sort of artisan winemaker you always hope to discover, a little disheveled, the cellar not quite up to Napa cleanliness. This was in Bué, a suburb of Sancerre, if you can even think of that concept.

But the new wines we tasted were superb, the vintner sensing my enthusiasm and moving from barrel to barrel, always from excellent to better. Just as merchant friends had confirmed my own experience, in small operations where the winemaker knows his wines barrel by barrel, he allows you to progress up the line only if you have gained his confidence.

I believe I did that, but something strange was happening to me. I was becoming woozier and woozier, even though I was following standard practice in spitting each sample. I eventually had to excuse myself, and on leaving the cellar, promptly fainted for the first and only time in my life. My travel companions, fortunately nearby, revived me in the cold clear Loire Valley air. What had happened was that the cellar was rich with carbon dioxide from wines still fermenting in barrel, a condition to which the vintner was accustomed on a daily basis, but which to a visitor was a blow to the senses.

No harm done, and an excellent Loire Valley dinner followed.

## ⌐ On First Meeting Hugh Johnson ⌐

I first met Hugh Johnson, so to speak, in Taipei in 1971. I was in Taiwan on business, and I shamelessly took advantage of the country's refusal to accept international copyright convention by purchasing several pirated books, among them Johnson's *Wine* (1967), that for perhaps two dollars. I avidly read the book cover to cover, seeking to improve my knowledge, and reflecting on what a long and marvelous life in wine this gentleman must have had, notably as secretary of the International Wine & Food Society and right hand to the famed André Simon.

Not many years later, when I had just begun professionally in wine and Johnson had recently authored *The World Atlas of Wine*, the single most important book in anyone's wine library, I called him in planning a London trip to inquire if we might have lunch. He readily agreed and specified one of his favorite restaurants, Wiltons.

I arrived a little before Johnson, and reflected on the seamless artistry of the service and also on the clientele, whose forebears had clearly been dining at Wiltons since the doors opened in 1742, if not at the nearby clubs, and who surely obtained their shirts from Turnbull & Asser or Hilditch & Key a short stroll away.

# Corks & Forks

I was expecting someone like the elder Alistair Cooke, but Johnson bounded in the door with "Sorry I'm late!" It turned out he was just four years my senior, which made him thirty-five at the time. He had simply gotten a head start on me in the wine arena.

Wiltons has always been primarily noted for seafood and game, and since grouse was just in season, that's what we chose. Hugh graciously asked me to select the wine, and I thought a reliable Châteauneuf-du-Pape would be about right. But when I tasted, I saw that the wine was raisiny, oxidized, spoiled. I asked for another bottle, and it showed the same defects. At this point, Hugh said "Robert, this tastes all right to me. I come here all the time, and I'd prefer not to make an issue." So I asked him to choose something else, which was delicious.

So here I've embarrassed Hugh Johnson, whom I had just met, in his favorite restaurant. But as our eventually cheery lunch wound down, the manager of Wiltons came to the table and asked, "Which of you gentlemen ordered your first two wines, and returned them?" I confessed.

"Well, sir, you did me a great favor. I tasted from both bottles and they were spoiled. Someone had stored them and other bottles carelessly on top of refrigeration, where they overheated. I wouldn't have known. Thank you."

Hugh and I exchanged smiles and have remained solid friends ever since.